"Is It Done Yet?"

"Is It Done Yet?"

Teaching Adolescents the Art of Revision

Barry Gilmore

HEINEMANN
Portsmouth, NH

Heinemann
A division of Reed Elsevier Inc.
361 Hanover Street
Portsmouth, NH 03801–3912
www.heinemann.com

Offices and agents throughout the world

The author and publisher wish to thank those who have generously given permission to reprint borrowed material:

Excerpts from *Engaged Writers and Dynamic Disciplines* by Chris Thaiss and Terry Myers Zawacki. Copyright © 2006 by Chris Thaiss and Terry Myers Zawacki. Published by Heinemann, a division of Reed Elsevier Inc., Portsmouth, NH. All rights reserved.

Library of Congress Cataloging-in-Publication Data
Gilmore, Barry.
  Is it done yet? : teaching adolescents the art of revision / Barry Gilmore.
      p. cm.
   ISBN-13: 978-0-325-01096-0 (alk. paper)
   ISBN-10: 0-325-01096-X
   1. English language—Composition and exercises—Study and teaching (Secondary). 2. Language arts (Secondary). I. Title.
   LB1631.G468 2007
   808'.0420712—dc22   2006037729

Editor: Lisa Luedeke
Production service: Denise Botelho
Production coordinator: Sonja S. Chapman
Cover design: Cat & Mouse Design, Catherine Hawkes
Author photograph: Ethan Sandifer
Compositor: SPi Publisher Services
Manufacturing: Steve Bernier

Printed in the United States of America on acid-free paper
11 10 09 08 07 EB 1 2 3 4 5

Contents

Foreword

To Revise or Not to Revise

Question: How many Therapists does it take to screw in a
        lightbulb?
Answer: One, but the bulb has to want to change.

This joke could also apply to an English teacher who desires to teach revision and meets the familiar refrain, "It's done." No amount of arm twisting, homework assigning, minilesson modeling, or just plain old-fashioned nagging can make that student change their opinion of that piece of writing. The student has to want to change it and writing teachers need to step back and find creative ways to grow that want on a daily basis. Barry Gilmore's funny and wise book *"Is it Done Yet?" Teaching Adolescents the Art of Revision* is a great place to start this exciting journey.

Early in the book Barry Gilmore examines the unconscious ways teachers impede revision. They grade papers too early in the process—they insist students revise a paper when the student sees no reason—they confuse revision with editing. He then shows concrete ways teachers can overcome these hurdles and start creating a classroom atmosphere where revision can thrive. From tips on peer conferences to guidelines on running writing workshop groups, to ideas for separating content revision from grammatical revision, or tips on how to deal with state assessment essays, Gilmore positions himself as both coach and cheerleader for English teachers grappling with the complex demands of the modern English teaching classroom.

Later chapters in the book extend Gilmore's practical revision tips to reader-response, fiction and poetry and line-by-line editing. Using examples of student work and published writing he not only tells teachers what to do but shows them how it looks on the page. This is the kind of teaching that sticks because it's got the "show" along with the "tell." But don't be fooled by all this great advice. Gilmore's job is not to show you how to make your students revise their work. In Chapter 1 he tells us firmly: **The writing teacher's job,**

ultimately, is not to revise for students but to teach students how to revise for themselves.

Beyond all the wise and practical advice Gilmore offers, there is another reason why I love this book—it's funny and fun to read. Though the author writes with great authority, he never places himself above the reader. Indeed, he uses humorous anecdotes from his personal life and classroom to humble himself and create a sense of joy even as he tackles a subject of dread for most English teachers. One of my favorite moments in the book is in Chapter 1 where Gilmore imagines the young Billy Shakespeare's first writing conference. It got me thinking of what Hamlet's soliloquy may have sounded like had it been about the subject of this book. I end this foreword with my version that I dedicate to all teachers who take Barry Gilmore's challenge to help students learn to revise for themselves like the young Danish prince.

> To revise
> Or not to revise
> That is the question.
> Whether tis nobler to suffer
> The slings and arrows of outrageous rubrics
> Or take arms against a sea of gradebooks
> > And by opposing flunk out.
> To fail, to drop, to leave
> No more and by our leaving say we end
> The homework and the thousand unnatural shocks
> That school is heir to,
> Tis a consummation devoutly to be wished
> To fail, to leave,
> To leave, perchance to write
> > Aye there's rub
> For after that writing
> Of the 1st draft
> what new dreams may come
> When we have shuffled
> Off this verbal coil,
> Must give us pause
> There's the calamity
> That makes revision worth it.

Barry Lane

Acknowledgments

Many thanks are due to the students and teachers who contributed their work and ideas to this book, but two of the teachers I most admire merit particular mention here as well as in the text: Bill Brown, my former teacher, and Dr. Sue Gilmore, my mother, who have each also served as a patient mentor, a colleague, and a reader. My wife, Susanna, not only continues to allow me to use her as a metaphor but is also my greatest source of support. Finally, thanks to Sonja Chapman, Denise Botelho, and especially Lisa Luedeke—who shepherded this volume through the process from idea to print.

1 *Getting to Carnegie Hall*

Is There a System?

I love being a writer. What I can't stand is the paperwork.
—Peter de Vries

Imagine that you're William Shakespeare's English teacher. Forget, for the moment, that the young Shakespeare had an actual teacher, Thomas Jenkins, whose idea of high-stakes testing probably included flogging boys who forgot the genitive plural of Latin nouns; forget that the rules of the English language were still in flux in the late sixteenth century. Will Shakespeare walks into your class today—you're his teacher.

The conversation might go something like this:

YOU: Billy, I asked you to revise your written assignment! Why didn't you do it?

WILL: I *did*.

YOU: But it isn't any different.

WILL: Sure it is. Look right there. I fixed the spelling of "bodkin."

YOU (reading Will's paper): "Who would put up with it all when he could just kill himself with a bare bodkin?" What about my note out here in the margin asking you to expand the ideas here? Did you see how I suggested that you specify what you mean by "putting up with it all"—what is it that you have to put up with? I wrote you a whole paragraph of comments on this section!

WILL: I know. But I couldn't think of anything else to say. Besides, I fixed everything that was, you know, *wrong*.

YOU: Yes, but this piece could be really good if you'd just work on it more. Someone might even want to perform it for you someday.

WILL: Yeah, right. Can I go now? I have to go change into my other tights for fencing practice . . .

Who knows? Maybe Shakespeare's first drafts were really lousy. Maybe Hamlet originally began this speech with the line, "The question is whether or not to be." Maybe Juliet initially lamented Romeo's departure by saying,

"Parting is really, really, sad." Maybe it took twelve drafts for the bard to expand the previous bit about the bodkin into this:

> For who would bear the whips and scorns of time,
> The oppressor's wrong, the proud man's contumely,
> The pangs of despised love, the law's delay,
> The insolence of office and the spurns
> That patient merit of the unworthy takes,
> When he himself might his quietus make
> With a bare bodkin?

Young Will misses the point; many students do. It's a cardinal rule for most English teachers, one I've wished I could tattoo backwards on to the foreheads of some of my students so they'd see it each time they look in the mirror, especially those who never seem to care that I've written any responses to the ideas in their papers, but who dutifully correct the most microscopic errors and return a clean copy of an essay thinking that it now constitutes a "final draft."

The rule is this: **Revising does not mean "fixing" mechanical errors.**

Professional writers know this rule as well as English teachers do, and they know that there's an even worse truth lying in wait for those who discover what revision really entails: **Ultimately, revision is almost entirely up to the author.** This book, for instance, has passed before the discerning and helpful eyes of a content editor, a production editor, a copy editor, a proofreader, several of my colleagues—even my mom, whose teaching career spans just about my whole life. All made suggestions, all contributed feedback and ideas and corrections, but the real revision took place before any of them ever read a word. The real revision took place when I threw out the first six drafts of this introductory chapter. Much of the real revision even took place in my head before I ever put a word on the page. Revision is a skill as much as a process, one that we learn from reading, writing, writing again, reading some more, and figuring out how to do it all better the next time. We could rephrase the rule above for teachers in this way: **The writing teacher's job, ultimately, is not to revise for students but to teach students how to revise for themselves.**

Ah, as young Will might say. There's the rub.

I can hear you now: *Revision's a pain. How can you even get students to* want *to revise, much less learn to do it for themselves?*

It's tricky, I admit. And let's face it—I could keep adding rules like those above, and the task of teaching revision might seem more and more daunting. Consider what we all know:

Good writers read. They read a lot.

Good writers *care* about what they write.

Good writers know that they have to write differently for different audiences.

No matter how hard good writers work at revision, they're rarely, if ever, completely satisfied with what they produce.

Daunting, isn't it? Okay, let's add that one, too: **Teaching others to write well is not easy.**

But you didn't become a teacher because it was easy, did you?

No, I did it for the money.

Yeah, right. Now pull the other leg. Seriously, let's try it through a metaphor:

My wife is a classical violinist, a pretty good one; she plays first chair in our city's symphony orchestra. People speculate all the time that it must be great to live with her; I get to hear all that wonderful music when she practices—and she does practice, all the time. But you know what I get to hear? Scales. Lots of scales. Or one passage of about three notes played over and over again at an agonizingly slow tempo. Or a bow technique practiced repeatedly with a single note. Or, sometimes, the sound of a music stand being kicked across the room out of frustration.

Now imagine a young person who doesn't even think she's particularly good at music, who doesn't think she has any talent, and envision telling her that this is what it takes to become fluent on the instrument—not just playing songs, not just performing, but routine attention to the minute details of playing—that the old joke about asking a New York cab driver how to get to Carnegie Hall ("practice, practice, practice") is right on the money. Imagine that you're put in the position of responding when the young player either puts down the instrument in disgust or decides it's okay just to go on scratching out the same horrible sounds over and over, without ever improving or learning anything new. What do you say?

Oh well, the violin's not for everyone?

Maybe. But there are two problems with this approach:

1. Writing *is* for everyone.
2. Giving up is a pretty weak life strategy. If you don't believe me, go try to find one—just one—adult who is completely happy that he or she gave up playing an instrument as a child, even if he or she was never going to end up anywhere near the stage at Carnegie Hall.

But you also don't just learn to practice the way my wife does on your own. You aren't just born with a musical ear, a knowledge of both technical skills and artistic approaches, and a compendium of practice routines, strategies, or methods. You learn those, and when you learn an effective strategy, a method that works for you, when your playing improves and you get the recognition you deserve for your accomplishment, you learn another rule, too: **Getting better at something (including writing) increases your desire to do it.**

And teachers who watch students make this discovery learn that one of the rules should be modified: **Teaching others to write well is hard, but no one manages to write better without teachers.**

I often wonder how my wife's early teachers felt when she did, in fact, perform in a string quartet at Carnegie Hall.

Keep this in mind, too. From a study of college students conducted at George Mason University from 2001 to 2006, Chris Thaiss and Terry Myers Zawacki produced a list of recommendations for practice that closely mirrors some of my rules; they suggested, for instance, that "good college writing comes from what writers care about" and that "college writers move to proficiency through stages of development" (a more complete listing of Thaiss's and Zawacki's results appears at the end of this book). The last item on the list of results from their study is especially worth pointing out: "Students," they say, "credit responsive teachers for their growth as writers." Without teachers, no one, not even a budding Shakespeare, improves what he or she writes. And students know it.

And that, all jokes aside, is probably why you became a teacher.

WHAT WE'RE AIMING FOR: *Revision Goals for Student Writing*

Building on their research, Thaiss led a session at the 2005 National Council of Teachers of English annual convention in which he posed this question to participants: "What writing skills do college-bound students need to possess?" The teachers in the audience offered a variety of responses, which I've listed here. The categories are mine.

Content/Argumentation

- Consistency in answering the question(s) posed by the prompt
- The ability to craft an essay with a controlling idea or thesis
- The ability to argue an idea or opinion in a sustained manner along with the interpretation of a text
- Knowledge of how to include ample and appropriate evidence
- Knowledge of how to include relevant research
- The ability to read critically and grapple with intellectually challenging texts
- A desire to add something new to conversation
- The ability to discuss works outside of the canon
- A variety of tools and strategies for reaching various audiences

Writing Style

- The ability to write with authority and control
- An arsenal of descriptive words and details
- Mature and diverse language and syntax
- Mastery of grammar rules and writing conventions

Revision

- The ability and desire to revise one's own work
- An awareness that revision is not just correcting a paper
- The ability to achieve all items on this list in a second or third draft
- A system for revision

Technical Skills

- The ability to avoid plagiarizing
- Computer literacy skills
- Knowledge of documentation formats (including MLA rules)

For the result of a ten-minute brainstorming session, it's a pretty good list. Good enough, at least, for us to come to some conclusions. One is that writing and revising are not distinct practices; they blend into one another and share the same goals. Teaching revision is, in effect, teaching students to achieve all of the other items on the list, though it may take time, since **no paper or piece of writing is perfect in the form in which it is first written.**

Another conclusion: writing teachers (and teachers of revision) want a system, much as writers themselves often develop a system for revision. It need not be a system that dictates exact procedures to every individual or for every piece of writing identically—the system can be fluid and organic. But some system—any system—is better than the general instruction some students receive simply to "rewrite," with no specific directions about *how* that should be accomplished.

So, Is There a System?

Is there a system for revision?

Simply: yes.

And no. Because every writer, every student, every class is different, there's no one catch-all schedule for revision that can be applied to every piece of writing. One student may need help turning each thought into a complete sentence for a second draft; another may be trying to decide between using a metonymy or a synecdoche for effect in a conclusion. We don't want to create any unhealthy straightjackets for writers. What's more, different types of writing—creative, expository, professional—may require slight differences in focus and process.

But yes. Writing can be broken down into its parts, and so the diagnostic process becomes fairly straightforward: check the parts. Make sure each one is working order and, if it isn't, fix it, improve it, go and find another one—whatever you need to do to get the whole piece up and running.

Okay, you say. *But is there a system for* teaching *revision?*

Sure. Here's the simple version:

1. Find a good activity to get students to check each part of their writing, from parts of speech to parts of the essay;

2. Teach students to recognize the parts for themselves;

3. Help students find the parts of their writing that are frequently weak or strong;

4. Give students the tools to help them improve the parts on their own the next time around;

   and, of course,

5. Practice, practice, practice.

The more complicated version? That's what you'll find in the rest of this book. The organization of this material is straightforward. To begin with, you'll find chapters on helping students to improve the content and argument of a paper and the style of their writing. Then, you'll find strategies and activities you can use in class, tips for revising on-demand writing (such as an essay for AP or IB exams or the SAT), ideas for using technology as a revision tool, and some thoughts about helping students to revise creative writing.

Within the first two chapters, I've broken down the larger aspects of student writing—content and style—into smaller pieces. Each section comes with an introduction, sample student work, and strategies for the classroom. Appendices at the end of the book provide sample teaching plans and Thaiss's and Zawacki's recommendations for practice.

Remember, finally, that teaching revision is like practicing medicine: the ultimate goal is to render yourself unnecessary. In that sense, any book about revision is really a book about writing—what makes it work and how to get to what works quickly and efficiently. I want students to nail every item on the teachers' list the first time; I want them to write with such fluency and control that we forget they ever had to practice to get there. They won't all become the next Shakespeare, they won't all stand on the stage at Carnegie Hall—but by removing the mystique, the terror, and the drudgery from the process of writing and revising, we can at least help to ensure that they will continue to write and to learn.

2 *That's What It's All About*

Revising Content

Quick, write a paragraph.

What, you want something to write about? Need a starting phrase? Okay, here's a topic: Write a paragraph about why we ask students to write essays, anyway. If you can figure that one out and explain it clearly, extra credit. But really, you could write about anything: your first baseball game, the time a pet died, where your name comes from.

You're not doing it, are you? You have more questions: how it will be graded, how long it's supposed to be, whether or not you're allowed to use first person. Or maybe you have trouble getting started. Or maybe you just don't like writing. Or maybe you *still* don't know exactly what you're supposed to be writing about.

We've all been there, haven't we? Either on the giving end or the receiving end of that assignment, or possibly both. Maybe you've been given a topic but no context, or a context but no specific topic, or, worst of all, maybe some English teacher has slapped a rubric in front of you with all sorts of little boxes and numbers and warnings about syntax (which you're still not sure is a real word) and has told you to be creative. And then it sets in, the sense of panic you feel when you're supposed to produce something brilliant, and you just want to get it over with. So you write something—anything—hoping it will get a C, maybe; you'd be okay with that.

Or perhaps you fall to it with gusto, because you've always loved writing, and you try your very best, pouring your soul out about where your name came from. And then you get the paper back from your teacher, and you got a C, but even with the rubric you're not really sure why.

Or maybe you write the paragraph, turn it in, and that's it. You never see it or hear about it again, and you don't bother to bring it up because, well, really, what's the point? And besides, if you did bring it up, you'd probably just get another C.

What do all of these scenarios have in common? What's the link?

I make a lot of Cs?

Okay, maybe, but even if you made an A on every assignment—particularly if you made an A on every assignment, since teachers have a tendency to comment less on good papers than on bad ones—you might well retain that sense that completing a writing assignment is like navigating an obstacle course blindfolded. You're not sure what to write about, or what's expected of you, or where the assessment of your writing is coming from, or who, really, you're writing for, or why you're even bothering at all.

And then, to top it all off, your teacher hands the C paper back to you and tells you to revise.

I remember I used to get this sinking sensation in my gut every time we drove to my Aunt Virgie's house, a sort of emotionally induced nausea, because as much as I loved visiting Aunt Virgie, I knew that at lunch I'd face pimento cheese sandwiches, deviled eggs, and cooked spinach. At nine, I'd rather have eaten dirt; I think I tried to. Revision assignments, at their worst, are like that.

We must change the way students think of revision and the way some of us present it (I include myself). We must retract the message that revision and proofreading are synonymous, or that revision is just an extra step one undertakes after the assignment gets the actual grade, or that revision is only necessary for really bad writing. We must rewrite—*revise*—how we sometimes approach the writing process:

- Revision can't take place only after grades are assigned. I'd hate to have been graded on the first draft of this chapter, or this book, before I had a chance to reconsider my approach, get some input, and revise using the tools I've gathered over time. In fact, if you think about it, how often are professional writers or business people of any sort graded on a first draft?

- Students should not only have to rewrite papers when they make low grades. Rewriting only poor papers makes revision a punishment instead of a natural part of the writing process.

- Revision needs to live up to its name and allow writers to *see* the piece, to envision it, again. In other words, revision can't just be about corrections, or even just about improving the flow of words or the selection of details; it must take into account content first.

There's good news, though. Revision, treated as an ally and not a necessary evil, can help students get past some of the hurdles in the way of good writing: boredom, fear, and resignation. Offering students the tools to revise content, in particular, not only improves writing but the attitude of writers. Content revision encourages students to take pride in and care with what they write, to invest themselves in it before hacking it up in the name of syntax or grammar.

Sound lofty? Maybe, but unless you actually sat down and wrote that paragraph like I asked you to, you can probably see what I mean: too many students approach a new essay assignment like bit characters in horror movies who go into the attic alone. You know you're going to get hacked; you just don't know what dark corner the monster will jump out of this time. If it takes lofty ideas about the place of revision to get students to feel safe sorting through the junk in the attic and looking for treasures, I'll play the idealist. Heck, I'll say it again, more clearly: the process of revision, handled well, can make students *want* to write. Handled poorly, it can make them dread it.

So, revision is good. What's more, I think there's a pretty simple but necessary approach to revision, beginning with content. You only have to rent any DVD and watch the "deleted scenes" section to know that fundamental changes to the topic of stories, even the best stories, take place all the time. It just doesn't make sense to correct spelling or remove a dangling participle before you realize that the topic "Macbeth's Tragic Flaw: He Was a Muggle" just isn't working out.

Think of the steps of revision, like ice cream or an alien head, as a cone (see Figure 2–1). Unfortunately, students all too often start at the bottom of the cone, with the narrowest task rather than the broadest, or skip the first steps

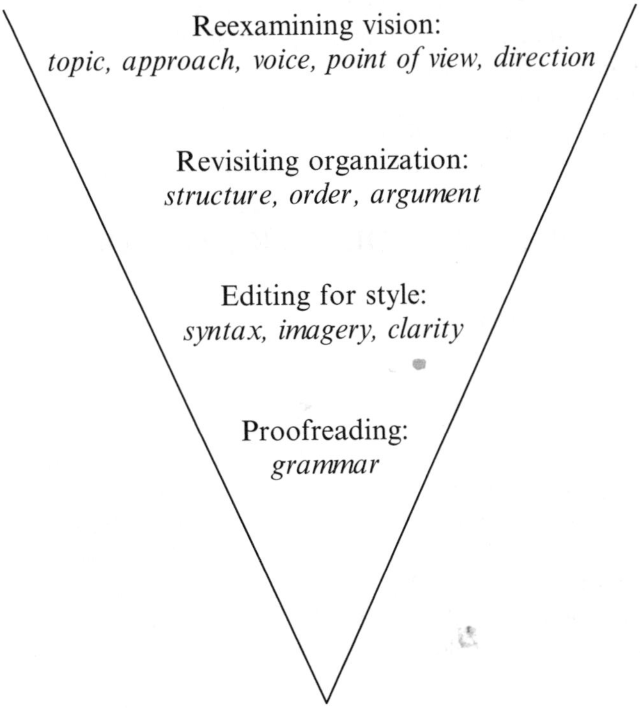

Reexamining vision:
topic, approach, voice, point of view, direction

Revisiting organization:
structure, order, argument

Editing for style:
syntax, imagery, clarity

Proofreading:
grammar

Figure 2–1 The Revision Cone

altogether. It's not that every topic needs reconsideration, but some topics might, as might tone or approach.

Put it in practical terms: imagine an assignment like the one I mentioned earlier, one that asks students to write a personal essay about where their names come from. Where would you start? I'd probably begin with a story; my dad thought my name sounded like a banker's, and he knew I'd be a banker. I write that down, and then spend an hour proofreading, maybe even editing.

The next day, I rethink my approach, and I go back, do a bit of research, and write about the meaning of my name. *Barry*, it turns out, is Gaelic for "fair-headed," according to one source, and comes from a French term for a javelin thrower, according to another, or, according to a third, it's a diminutive of the name Fionnbharr, all of which I'm glad my dad didn't know—can you imagine what profession he might have picked out for me with a name like that? In any case, I like all of this better than the banker bit, so I go back and revise pretty much my whole composition. My first draft goes out the window, along with an hour of tinkering that I might have spent, oh, balancing my checkbook, the closest I'll ever get to banking outside of hurling verbal abuse at the ATM in despair or teaching *The Merchant of Venice*.

Content comes first. In the process of revising what we write about, we ask good questions that determine how we write it at every level. And just possibly in the process we make a decision about point of view that has less to do with the requirements for getting an A than it does with our own satisfaction. We still need strategies for revision, and that's where the rest of this chapter comes in, but let's not lose sight of what's important: Revision is about making the words you write count, not counting to see if your number of words is right.

WHAT THE HECK ARE YOU TALKING ABOUT?: *Improving the Thesis*

> *Grasp the subject; the words will follow.*
> —Cato the Elder

True story: I'm writing three essay assignments for a senior English class on the board and one of my students—call her Maria—asks this question:

"Mr. G., where do you *get* all these essay topics from, anyway?"

I turn and point to my bookshelves. "There's this big book," I tell her. "*Ten Thousand Essay Topics for English Teachers*. They gave it to me when I was hired. I just look them up in there."

Here's the good part. Maria says, "Oh." Then she goes back to copying down the prompts from the board.

Oh.

Actually, it's not a terrible idea for a book, though I'm not sure I'd want to write it. And it's true that not all of the essay prompts I use come out of my own head; I've robbed resource books, pilfered from other teachers, cast back to my own high school assignments, modified prompts from AP essays, and even (confession coming) looked at the online study guides—you know, the ones we forbid our students to use—for good ideas. But the majority of the essay topics I assign are original.

What's troublesome is not that students like Maria don't give me credit for my work, but that it doesn't occur to them that essay topics are something you might think up for yourself. It's troublesome because I teach seniors who may, after twelve years of schooling, never have been asked to come up with an essay topic for themselves. It's troublesome because I believe that

- the ultimate goal of teaching students to write essays is to teach them to demonstrate their sophistication as readers and critical thinkers;
- sophisticated essays demand sophisticated topics; and
- sophisticated topics can't be handed to students; they must be developed, honed, and shaped by the author.

Or, if that seems too complicated, we can boil it down to this: **If we want students to write better essays, we must offer them a role in developing topics and thesis ideas.**

So revision starts here, possibly before a word ever arrives on the page, with the reconsideration of what a student is writing *about* and why.

Of course, there's more to an essay than a topic. A lot more. "Concepts of Love in *Romeo and Juliet*," for instance—that's a *topic*. We can turn it into a *theme* by adding a verb and a suggestion of what the author has to say about the topic: "It is possible to experience true love at first sight" or "Love cannot be deterred by the obstacle of social expectations" or "Love scenes are funny when the guy wears tights." See the difference? Once you're discussing a *theme*, there's always the possibility that your idea is not, in fact, a legitimate theme, that you're dead wrong—there's a burden of proof. That's why essays exist—to prove something. But who wants to prove something that everybody already knows? Who wants painstakingly to collect and present evidence to argue that *Romeo and Juliet* is just another tragedy, as if the five dead bodies weren't enough of a hint?

Let's take the first theme from the previous paragraph as a working example, the idea that *Romeo and Juliet* suggests that it is possible to experience true love at first sight. Can this idea be developed into a reasonable thesis? Sure. One might agree or disagree, and either way, there's ample evidence in the play to discuss and interpret and use as support for an argument. By the end of a beautiful fourteen-line sonnet smack in the middle of the Capulets' hoedown, the two lovers are either hopelessly in love or hopelessly infatuated or, perhaps, just hopeless. And, after all, if we're talking about love at first sight, the moment when Romeo and Juliet actually see one another is a reasonable place to start. Thus is born the typical thesis statement for a student essay. Here's Maria's, for instance:

> In William Shakespeare's play *Romeo and Juliet*, the two main characters, Romeo and Juliet, seem to fall in love at first sight. Throughout the play, issues of love are addressed by many characters. <u>By examining the scene in which the two characters meet, the balcony scene, and Juliet's first meeting with Paris, it can be proven that it is possible for characters in *Romeo and Juliet* to truly fall in love at first sight.</u>

If I'm lucky, Maria's paragraph is the sort of thing I get on the first essay of the year from students—she's learned, at least, that she needs a thesis statement; someone even taught her to underline it, just to prove to herself that it's there. (She'll have to unlearn that practice before taking an AP exam, because doing so may a) insult a reader who feels pretty capable of finding the thesis statement and b) suggest that Maria's thesis is so simple it can easily be contained in one sentence—read on for more about that idea.) Many first paragraphs aren't as logical as Maria's, many throw in more extraneous and boring information ("Love is defined by *Webster's Dictionary* as . . ."), and some have nowhere near this level of grammatical confidence, the split infinitive and use of passive voice notwithstanding.

Still, you can almost see the gears working in Maria's head, can't you? The item that will certainly become the topic of the fourth paragraph—the meeting between Juliet and Paris—smacks of desperation; Maria knows she needs a third example, but doesn't seem too confident. The paper will address a topic and a theme, sure, but in a formulaic manner that will provide the discussion with about as much depth as a cup of water.

Okay, you're thinking. *Weak thesis. So what does revision have to do with this?*

Glad you asked. To find the answer, let's back up and think about revising not just the final paper but even our process of getting there. First, let's consider how students might arrive at topics, and then we'll examine how those topics can be turned into a thesis and argument.

Weighing Your Options: The Role of Choice in Writing

Classrooms aren't democracies. Many wouldn't last long if they were (Can you imagine the vote on whether to discuss the line "to sleep, perchance to dream" or to act it out?). That doesn't mean we can't learn a few things from the democratic method, and the most important lesson may be this one: choice matters. Students who have a stake in what they study and write may do a better job of studying and writing.

If you're studying a specific work, such as *Romeo and Juliet*, some choices are limited. Although I'm a proponent of allowing students to choose their reading material (within limits) when possible, if the whole class is studying a work, the choice not to read that work has serious consequences, including failure. Other choices are easier to offer; essay topics are a good example.

You might reasonably worry that offering students that chance to develop their own essay topics raises other concerns: the process takes time, it opens the door for plagiarism, it requires some oversight, it's a bit worrisome for a teacher (What if the topics the students come up with just aren't very good?). I argue that it's worth it. Time is your ally; spending part of a class period early on developing a topic eliminates the need to plagiarize, and possibly *prevents* a student from plagiarizing—it's more difficult to find an online essay that addresses a specific, nuanced concern about a text than to find one that addresses a text's most obvious thematic elements. What's more, I've found that students eventually get used to the idea of developing essay topics, and as both the topics and the process improve students come to take more pride in and ownership of the entire essay-writing experience.

Here are a few tips to consider:

- Regard the step of topic choice as a part of the revision process, and spend time revising topics. Revision in its broadest sense—the rethinking and reevaluation of major ideas—is probably best done before writing begins in earnest, anyway. The development, discussion, refinement, further development, further discussion, and fine-tuning of a topic into a workable thesis may just be the most important step of revision you can teach a student.

- Use class time to your advantage. If students come up with topics and refine those topics in class, the chances that a draft will come from another source are minimized.

- Use homework to your advantage. Alternate class time and out-of-class assignments to give students a chance to think about a topic, work on necessary steps, and discuss it with others. Here's a model I suggest:

  1. As a class, brainstorm possible issues and topics to discuss. I sometimes make lists on the board or on poster-sized sheets around the room with aspects of a text that might be discussed: themes, symbols, setting, character development, language, and style.

  2. Take one or two of these issues and develop, with the class, some possible themes by adding a verb and making a statement. Then tell the students they can't use those statements, but they can develop similar statements using any of the other topics on the communal list.

  3. That night, as homework, have students find evidence from the text (or other sources, as appropriate) that address the theme they've chosen. Stress the importance of comprehensive evidence (from all parts

of a text, for instance) and the inclusion of evidence that might be contradictory or tangentially related to the idea.

4. Take ten or fifteen minutes out of another class period to have students in pairs or groups discuss the evidence and refine the theme into a thesis.

- Take the process of topic/thesis development step by step, allowing students time to reconsider, revise, and discuss with others.
- Have students write only the first paragraph of an essay, then have pairs or groups of students discuss each other's theses and possibilities for exploring shades of meaning.

I find that an important step in the process of creating a thesis, at least early on, is a period of discussion in which students can bounce ideas off one another, consider how others approach a similar problem, or simply think about the topic. Once students have committed to topics, I have them review and discuss the following list in an effort to broaden their possibilities for constructing thesis statements. I also suggest that a student consider this list when I decide the student is ready to expand a thesis on his or her own.

- *Proof.* What idea do quotations or scenes from a text (or similar evidence) offer? Are there any ambiguous or contradictory ideas embodied in the evidence? If so, how might one explain the ambiguity or contradiction?
- *Imagery.* What images are tied to the theme or used to convey it? Is there recurring diction or symbolism that appears in passages in which the theme is developed? What possibilities or problems do these images create?
- *Nuance.* Where are the gray areas in the idea? Where, in other words, are there lingering questions, no matter how strong a case one might make in support of an idea? The nature of texts, in particular, is such that black-and-white assertions rarely hold up—a tolerance for the ambiguity of ideas is often apparent in strong *essays*. If such ambiguities do exist, might the author's awareness and discussion of such gray areas *strengthen* the thematic idea?
- *Extension.* What connections might be made to other themes or ideas? How do those connections expand the original theme?

Yeah, it spells PINE. Whatever helps, right?

Even if you hand students an essay prompt, the steps for developing a thesis in response to that prompt are crucial. If every essay prompt you offer suggests three aspects of a five-paragraph essay, then you'll get five-paragraph essays covering those three points. That's okay, until you're ready for students to develop three points on their own, or better yet, to move beyond the form altogether.

Much of the process of revising content deals with a conundrum: we teach our students to write in forms that are rather like straitjackets, then try to get them to worm out of those same straitjackets. Reconsideration of these four areas, though, makes it easier to loosen the bonds of a form, like the standard five-paragraph essay, and to move toward a revision that takes into account a more sophisticated argument.

You Can Argue with Success: Revising Big Ideas

Students need formulae early on, and the process of getting them to follow those formulae is relatively straightforward: keep practicing the form over and over. By the time they get it, the formula may be so ingrained that it's hard for a student to imagine anything else.

Take Maria's introduction. It gets the essay going, but it's not particularly inspired. There's room for revision. Here's the first draft of her introduction, based on a topic she chose, again:

> In William Shakespeare's play *Romeo and Juliet*, the two main characters, Romeo and Juliet, seem to fall in love at first sight. Throughout the play, issues of love are addressed by many characters. By examining the scene in which the two characters meet, the balcony scene, and Juliet's first meeting with Paris, it can be proven that it is possible for characters in *Romeo and Juliet* to truly fall in love at first sight.

Another student, Tony, chose a topic similar to Maria's, so the next day in class I asked them to work as partners. Their instructions were simple: read the thesis statements in each introduction, then look over all of the available evidence one might use to support the thesis. In the process, Maria and Tony realized that there might be evidence that arose in the play *before* the scene in which Romeo and Juliet first meet. Their discussion, I imagine, went something like this:

TONY: Actually, there's a lot of talk about love in act one, before they ever meet. Check out this line: "Love is a smoke made with the fume of sighs; Being purged, a fire sparkling in lovers' eyes."

MARIA: I've got one from Romeo about eyes, too. Here it is: "Alas that love, whose view is muffled still, Should without eyes see pathway to his will!"

TONY: "Without eyes?" That sounds like he thinks you can fall in love without seeing.

MARIA: That doesn't fit what I'm saying. I'm saying you can fall in love when you first see someone.

TONY: Yeah, and this line that Juliet says is like that too: "If looking liking move." That means that she's not sure looking and liking go together, right?

MARIA: Okay, so there's all this stuff about eyes and seeing, but they don't seem to think it makes you fall in love. But at the ball it does seem like they fall in love just from looking at each other.

TONY: Maybe that's just in the movie.

MARIA: No, I really think it happens. Romeo's in love before he even talks to her.

TONY: Maybe he just *thinks* he's in love.

MARIA: Either way, it doesn't really agree with this stuff from act one, totally.

TONY: Well, it's different with Juliet, right? I mean, when they say this stuff back in act one, they haven't met each other yet. Maybe you can only fall in love at first sight with the right person, so they don't believe it until it happens.

MARIA: I like that. I'll work on that tonight.

TONY: We've got to do this tonight? Tonight?

MARIA: Tonight.

An idyllic conversation, I know. More likely, Tony and Maria spent most of their time talking about the upcoming school production of *West Side Story*, but something like this may take place in student groups. In Maria's case, something worked, because her revision included an awareness that some shift takes place in the play *before* the scenes she originally mentioned:

> A generally accepted idea about William Shakespeare's tragedy, *Romeo and Juliet*, is that the two young lovers fall in love as soon as they lay eyes on one another. But Juliet says in the first act, "I'll look to like, if looking liking move" (1.3.97). With this, she raises doubts about the possibility that love can be achieved only by what one sees. Throughout the play, in fact, references to the eyes and to seeing relate to the overall message about love and how characters approach it. In fact, these doubts about love at first sight make Romeo and Juliet's first meeting and almost instantaneous connection even more powerful, because it proves they've fallen in love quickly despite their feeling that it might not be possible to do so. Overall, Shakespeare's explorations of the visual aspects of love through scenes ranging from Juliet's first meeting with Paris to the famous balcony scene create the impression that Romeo and Juliet at least *feel* as if they have fallen in love at first sight, and may in fact have done so.

Even if Maria had stuck with three scenes in her last sentence instead of leaving open the possibility of discussing several scenes, there are more ideas in this paragraph—the connection to visual imagery, the development of the characters' attitudes, the balance between feeling and reality, and the possibility that by raising doubts early on, Shakespeare reinforces the power of a central scene—than can be contained easily in a standard five-paragraph essay. The thesis is sophisticated, even if the language is, for the most part, that of a student. Maria can revisit how she incorporates the quotation or her syntax later; the most important point, first, is the quality of her argumentation.

On this assignment, Maria proved that she learned this lesson: the argument of an essay may not be one you always win or lose, but a good argument is a little bit like love at first sight—it takes you by surprise, but it just feels right.

BETWEEN THE LINES: *Revising Less Than an Essay*

Back to that paragraph, the one from the introduction to this chapter. Here's a sample from a student given just the assignment I described—the task of writing about her own name:

> The correct way to pronounce my name is "a'-kee-eh," with the last "e" being the short e. Each syllable is pronounced distinctly and sharply without blending into the next syllable. Unfortunately, when people try to pronounce it "in the right way," they actually mispronounce it by creating a whole different word, sound, and meaning: *a'-ki-ya*, which means an "empty house" in the Japanese language. In my opinion, being "a key" is better than the alternative, "empty house," because *akie* derives from the word *aki*, which in Japanese means *autumn*, the best season of the year! Even though the pronunciation of autumn *aki* is different from the English words "a key" (the ending /ee/ sound of the word *aki* is not prolonged), I am willing to compromise and choose to be "a key"—to lock the door of an empty house.
>
> —*Akie Maekawa*

English was Akie's second language, one she didn't learn until she was in middle school. Writing, one might say, was her third language, because she had to learn from scratch the vocabulary and systemized approaches we teach students in language arts classes. A five-paragraph essay? Akie had never heard of such a thing. But given a topic she'd obviously thought about before and given time in which to write, Akie was able to produce this paragraph.

It's never simple. If we deconstruct writing too much, students will fall into the trap of writing what they think we want to hear, and instead of Akie's personal statement we wind up with a stiff and prosaic essay like this:

continued

> Names are a very important part of one's personality. The name Sarah, for instance, comes from the Bible. This shows that names have a long tradition for many people. Tradition helps to determine the adult one becomes.

But if we *don't* deconstruct writing, we may end up with something illogical, too short, or off-topic.

I'd argue that one of the most important jobs falls to teachers who instruct students in writing less than an essay—paragraphs, short compositions, book reports and book reviews, or even journals. These teachers have the responsibility (and the opportunity) to teach students to find a voice, to write logically, to organize their thoughts, and above all, to figure out how to harness their natural ability to say something important and stylize it without turning it into the stiff, dull prose that's all too often thought of as "writing." What's surprising is not that these teachers sometimes fail, but that they sometimes succeed—even so, the goal has to be to succeed every time, with every student who has something to say.

Akie moves, in her paragraph, from information to reflection, from shorter sentences to longer sentences, from a simple idea (the pronunciation of her name) to variations on that idea (the ways it gets mispronounced) to a combination and personal statement about those ideas (her willingness to compromise). The second example I included, by "Sarah," is constructed according to a precise formula suggested by a college composition book on my bookshelf; the formula insists on a topic sentence, a specific example, an explanation of the example (repeat as necessary), and a concluding idea. Which one do you like better?

I'm not suggesting that teachers should never give students structure, or ideas for construction of paragraphs and essays, or even formulae. I'm not suggesting we just throw out a topic and let students fend for themselves.

I *am* suggesting that there are ways to harness the natural desire students have to say something worthwhile. Consider, for instance, the following instructions for revision once students have written a paragraph or longer assignment:

- *Use reverse outlining.* Deconstruct the paragraph sentence by sentence into an outline that states what each sentence *does*, not what it says. If the outline makes sense, the paragraph probably does, too. Then ask these questions: How else might I have arranged this paragraph? Could I have started or ended differently? Could I have expanded on my examples? If I were to write a second paragraph, how could I make the organization different?

- *Reflect*:
  - What is the most surprising or unique thing about this paragraph?
  - How could a reader tell that I, not anyone else, wrote this paragraph, even if it isn't about me?
  - Is there a twist—a counterargument, a new idea, a surprising sentence, a joke—somewhere in this paragraph? If there isn't, should there be?
  - Does this paragraph get somewhere, or does it just repeat the same idea again and again?
  - Have I written about something interesting and worthwhile? Does anyone care about this?
  - What's the best thing about what I just wrote?

- *Talk it out.* Before writing, ask your students a question and record their oral answers. Then ask them to write a response. Compare the results—besides the fact that students are fascinated by their own voices, the contrast in the details a student chooses to include might be striking.
- *Draw it.* Trust me, I'm no artist. My stick figures look arthritic and every animal I draw looks like a cross between a cow and an octopus. But I draw all the time, because many students learn and remember visually. It works with writing, too—students might include details, descriptions, examples, and images in their visual work that they'd never have thought to include in a written paragraph. Drawing also offers an entry point—a place to start other than an abstract or overly generalized introductory sentence.

Eventually, students will learn to fit paragraphs together logically into a larger argument. Look at this paragraph, from a later essay Akie wrote about *An Enemy of the People*:

In this play the conflict involves family relations: the protagonist Dr. Stockmann single-handedly fights his brother Mayor Peter Stockmann and the public in matters concerning contaminated bath waters. Dr. Stockmann is the only one truly concerned with the well-being of others, specifically the sick and the elderly, who visit the bath houses in hopes of recovering from various sicknesses. His opponent is

continued

society, which is as contaminated as the filthy bath water; only, his society is contaminated with corruption and lies: "all the sources of our *moral* life are poisoned and that the whole fabric of our civic community is founded on the pestiferous soil of falsehood" (Ibsen 187). Dr. Stockmann's determination and moral obligation to his community do not allow him to struggle emotionally in deciding which side to take: "there was one thing I wished for—eagerly, untiringly, ardently—and that was to be able to be of service to my native town and the good of the community" (188). But the right choice is not always popular.

Here, Akie's paragraph, part of a much longer analysis, actually follows pretty closely the formula from that college composition guide. The difference? Akie couldn't have gotten here in a straight line from that formula. She had to learn to write organically, to put ideas together as they made sense to her, to revise the content of what she wrote on a smaller scale. Akie grappled, in writing this paper, with some big issues: the struggle between conscience and expectation, the difficulty of choosing between family and conviction. She also struggled with how to express these ideas in logical, rational order. She got there through revision, through practice in paragraph after paragraph, through assignments smaller than an essay, through writing about her name, but not by following a formula.

THROUGHOUT HISTORY . . . *Revising Introductions*

The last thing one knows in constructing a work is what to put first.
—Blaise Pascal

Here's the dirty little secret we rarely tell students about the typical introductory paragraph of an essay: except for the thesis statement, nothing in it is important.

That's not the way it should be, but the message students too often get is that the introduction can be filled with fluff and filler, so long as there's a clear thesis there somewhere. So sure, introductions bring up the topic, name an author, identify a title. But more often than not, introductions by students also compress about a million years of human history into a bland and unsupported generalization:

Since the dawn of man, humans have waged a war between their passions and their personal responsibilities.

Even if the topic doesn't sound familiar, the type of sentence should. In this case, I actually wrote that sentence in tenth grade for an assignment my English teacher, Mr. Kaplan, made. And then, between this sentence and my eventual thesis statement, came four sentences of complete B.S.:

> *Antigone*, by Sophocles, was written thousands of years ago, yet its lessons ring true today. The title character is Antigone, Creon's niece. Because Antigone must decide whether to follow Creon's law or her own conscience, the play is an excellent example of passion vs. duty. This conflict is common in much literature, but nowhere is it more clearly exemplified than in this excellent play.

Man, if I'd been Mr. Kaplan, I'd have resented a student like me for wasting an entire two minutes of my life.

That's not what Mr. Kaplan did. One of the best teachers I've ever known, he patiently helped me work out for myself that there are better ways to introduce a topic than this redundant and unsupported approach. Then, on the last day of my senior year of high school, Mr. Kaplan handed me a folder containing all of the drafts of every essay I'd ever written in a high school English class. I'm still not sure what he had in mind. Should I have felt inspired? Nostalgic? Thankful? Determined to succeed in college?

Or maybe he meant me to feel exactly what I do when I look back through that folder, which I still keep in my classroom: abject humiliation. I call the folder, in fact, "The Humiliator." I talk about it to my students:

"You think *your* introduction to that *Jane Eyre* essay was lousy? Let's check out what I wrote in The Humiliator."

Actually, my essay on *Jane Eyre* was really, really terrible. But Mr. Kaplan didn't rip it apart; instead he focused on my introduction. Why? Because he knew, then, that if I could nail the introduction, if I could figure out what was worth saying and what wasn't, the rest of the essay would fall into place. Every now and then, when students complain that they just don't write well or that I don't understand what it's like ("You write *books*," they say to me, as if that means I've never composed a poorly written sentence), I pull out The Humiliator and read them just the opening line of that essay about *Jane Eyre*:

> Throughout history and during the nineteenth century, men and women fell in love.

Gosh, you think?

Mr. Kaplan probably would have been within his rights to lock *me* in an attic for writing that sentence. He knew, I suspect, that sometimes students have to write full introductions before they revise to discover *good*, full introductions. And he knew that revising content meant getting to that good introduction.

Many teachers suggest that introductions should work like funnels, moving from the broad to the specific (and conclusions should do the opposite); others suggest beginning with a rhetorical question, a quotation, or a definition. I'm not against any strategy that works for a given student, but I also don't believe that an introduction *must* do anything other than hook the reader and lay out the argument.

And that's the problem: when we give students a tip for hooking the reader, like starting with a dictionary entry, we all too often rob introductions of anything that really makes them gripping. Sooner or later we must confront the inescapable reality: the introductions of many essays are boring, stiff, and largely extraneous. And there's a deeper problem rooted in this one; students may come to believe that introductions *should* be stiff. They'll start to begin personal essays and even fiction just like they begin their essays, as if every piece of writing should mire its audience in the muddiest of generalizations quickly and fully.

To see what I mean, let's take a look at the personal essay first.

Making the Cut: Introducing Personal Writing

Actually, personal essays and stories often have an easy fix for a bogged-down introduction: cut the first paragraph. It's remarkable how often this advice works. Look at the opening of this first draft, for example, written about a significant person in the author's life:

> She has shaped my character, my responses to my surroundings, and my outlook on my own method of existence. She has almost been removed from my life and from the world around us twice by circumstances out of her control, yet she has taught me that one must maintain a positive outlook on life and has refused to be beaten.
>
> —*Phoebe Fraser*

Phoebe's getting at something, but it's not clear just what. There's a story we're not being told, and while I'm mildly curious to know what that story is, I wouldn't have much trouble putting this essay down. If the story came more quickly and with specifics, I might change my mind. In Phoebe's revision, she cut the above paragraph and began with the second:

> I was a bossy, precocious three-year-old with a sizeable vocabulary and an unceasing desire to talk when I was informed that my mother had a "spot in her head" that needed "fixing." Later on, I learned that my mother had suffered from a large tumor in the right frontal lobe of her brain which needed to be removed through a particularly invasive procedure known as a craniotomy.

As difficult as Phoebe's situation is, this is a story I want to hear. I already care about this precocious three-year-old and her mother. And once Phoebe earns that care from her audience, she can go back and insert some of the more abstract reflection—in the conclusion.

Begin at the point at which things change, a writing teacher once told me. It's not bad advice for personal essays. Move the action up, right to the top of the page. Earn the opportunity to reflect. If there's no action to move up, make some. That's what revision is for.

And Now . . . Introducing the Formal Essay

I can hear you: *You can't just start in medias res with a formal essay. There's got to be an introduction.*

True. But the introduction needn't drag like a Ford Pinto in the mud, either. What students *can* do is step back after writing a first draft, breathe deeply, and ask some important questions about the opening paragraph:

1. Who is the audience for the paper? What does the audience know and what does it need to know?

2. What important information have I included? What information is extraneous to my point?

3. What can be supported with proof and what can't? Have I provided the proof? Do I need more evidence? Am I generalizing just to fill space?

4. Does every piece of information or idea in the introduction lead logically to the next?

By way of example, let's look at the first essay I received from a senior who would go on to become our school's valedictorian, Aditi. Here's the introduction to that first essay:

In the general body of literature, characters are created in such a manner as to educate the reader in some manner based on how they deal with and rectify their individual flaws. One of the most prevalent issues considered is the influence of pride, which impairs the character's judgment and prevents rational thought. Teiresias observed that all men are flawed, yet the only obstacle to overcome in rectifying their flaws is the presence of this pride. In Jhumpa Lahiri's *The Namesake*, the protagonist, Gogol Ganguli, the child of first generation Indian immigrants in Boston, must overcome his overwhelming sense of pride and acknowledge his roots and past over the course of the novel, despite his ardent denial of his tradition. Through observation of his changing relationship with his name, the development of his pride, his complete denial of his roots, and his final acknowledgement of his past, his pride becomes extremely evident.

—*Aditi Balakrishna*

Let's leave aside for a moment the first of the four questions I posed—the one about audience—we'll return to it in time. Instead, let's consider the other three.

Is there any extraneous information? Sure. The reference to Teiresias, unless it has some more significant role in the entire argument, is pretty extraneous, no matter how wise he was.

Are there unsupported generalizations? The first sentence certainly fits this bill.

Does every piece of information lead logically to the next? Actually, the paragraph is fairly logical. Teiresias comes out of nowhere, but Aditi doesn't suddenly veer off and discuss something completely unrelated, like a historical event that happened to take place while the novel was written but that had no direct influence on the author.

Still, what would be lost by taking a note from our approach to personal essays, and cutting the first three sentences entirely? What would we miss if the essay got to the point right away?

> In Jhumpa Lahiri's *The Namesake*, the protagonist, Gogol Ganguli, the child of first generation Indian immigrants in Boston, must overcome his overwhelming sense of pride and acknowledge his roots and past over the course of the novel, despite his ardent denial of his tradition. Through observation of his changing relationship with his name, the development of his pride, his complete denial of his roots, and his final acknowledgement of his past, his pride becomes extremely evident.

It's tighter, certainly. The thesis is clear. It's only two sentences.

Only two sentences?

Well, they're pretty good sentences. And I'd rather read two like these than five that don't really say anything. But if Aditi were to go back and question that thesis, to ask about possible proof, imagery, nuances, and extensions, what might happen then? Maybe something like this, her eventual final revision, in which she shows that she's thought more deeply about Gogol's "relationship with his name" and "denial of his roots":

> Gogol Ganguli, the protagonist in Jhumpa Lahiri's *The Namesake*, is a prime example of a character seeking to redefine his racial identity in two dimensions—through separation from the immigrant group he is obligated to be a part of and subsequent acceptance into mainstream American society, where he has always felt more comfortable. However, Gogol's journey to define himself is far more complex than simply separation and acclimation—in fact, these two processes are inextricably intertwined, represented by the motifs of his cultural identity and his name respectively. The name Gogol itself holds significance in that it is a relic of a part of Gogol's father's past, a bond with a famous writer, and a reminder of his Bangladeshi heritage, and through his relationship with this name Gogol must overcome his pride and, finally, acknowledge his roots.

Go back and look at Aditi's first draft; even if you haven't read *The Namesake*, you'll see how much more effectively Aditi's going to cover the thematic territory of the novel. If you look closely, you'll see, too, that Aditi has grappled successfully with the first of our four questions, the one I said we'd come to—the question of audience.

Are You Talking to Me? *Considering Audience*

Aditi faced a dilemma in writing this introduction that I'm not sure many students solve. On the one hand, she knew I'd read this novel; on the other, she knew a classmate or two who hadn't read the novel would help edit her essay. From there, it only gets more complicated: one of Aditi's teachers, at some point in the past, told her to write the essay as if the teacher "knew absolutely nothing." Another told her she had too much plot summary, but she'd put it in the essay because she was pretending the teacher, who "knew absolutely nothing," needed some context for the discussion. Then along came practice essays for the AP English exam in eleventh and twelfth grades, with readers who may or may not have read *The Namesake*—who could tell? And, beyond that, the real problem: what was she writing essays *for*, anyway? Were they supposed to be like the literate but mainstream book reviews in, say, the *New Yorker*, or like academic books that started out as someone's dissertation, or as some other genre of writing Aditi hadn't even encountered yet? What were the models for this sort of essay supposed to be, or were there any? Was the essay just an end in itself, like making a sketch for a painting you'd never see on a canvas?

And if Aditi actually asked me all of those questions, what would my answer be? *All of the above* just doesn't seem to cut it. To make matters worse, since introductions generally set the tone and purpose of the essay, it's an issue a student must confront early in the writing process.

Ultimately, Aditi compromised. Gogol Ganguli, she tells us in her final version of the paragraph, is the novel's protagonist. She's decided she doesn't need to define him as "the child of first generation Indian immigrants in Boston." She also slips the word *protagonist* into a necessary subordinate clause, so it's no longer a main point. She's no longer saying, "Look, this is the protagonist, which you need to know because I have to treat you like an imbecile;" now she's saying, "We both know he's the protagonist; let's mention it but not make a big deal of it, okay?"

Maybe such compromises are the best students can do. But I think we owe it to students to be a little clearer on the subject. Who is the audience? Why are we asking them to write this way? Why can't they use first person, or if they can, why is that suddenly okay when it wasn't for so many years? And, most importantly of all, what do the students themselves think they're writing these pieces for?

For what it's worth, here's how I deal with this issue in my own classroom:

- Early in the year, we read and discuss two examples of professional literary analysis—a review from a respected source and a critical essay on a work we're reading. We look particularly at the introduction (or first few paragraphs) and discuss how the authors handle audience—what assumptions they make, what information they provide, and what tone they adopt.

- When making assignments, I try to suggest a potential (hypothetical or real) audience for the piece. Before long, students don't need to have the discussion for assignments I've made several times, like formal essays, but the discussion is helpful early on.

- I try to *provide* an audience some of the time. The audience might come in many forms: I have peer groups read essays, I ask students to have a parent or adult friend read an essay, I post essays on bulletin boards or share them with other classes, and I've even managed to convince other teachers to read and discuss essays with students (without grading them— you'd be surprised how great the math teacher who teaches next door to me is at reading and discussing student writing). In each case, I discuss with students where their responsibility to their audience lies—how much they need to explain and how much they can assume an audience knows. Of course, when there's an actual future audience for the paper, as with college admissions or AP essays, we have similar discussions.

- For essays that only I am likely to read, I set some ground rules. Students should assume I've read the work, and therefore I need absolutely no plot summary. They should also assume that I have a basic knowledge of how literature works—of literary terms, devices, and analytic strategies. I don't need to hear, in other words, the definition of a simile. What they should not assume, for the purposes of their writing, is that I've *thought* about this particular work very deeply (even if I have); every idea and connection should be explained carefully and clearly, without assumptions. Finally, they should assume that I am a competent critical reader, and that I will be able to consider their argument and ask critical questions, make connections, and create counterarguments—in fact, they can be sure I'll do just that if they don't do it themselves.

The result of such discussions, I hope, is that when students like Aditi identify "the protagonist, Gogol Ganguli, the child of first generation Indian immigrants in Boston," they do so intentionally, for a particular audience. The result, for introductions, is usually a tighter, more focused opening that translates into greater awareness of voice, tone, and purpose.

More Ideas for Revising Introductions

Here are a few more tips for helping students prepare introductions:

- One of my favorite critical essays to use as an example is J. R. R. Tolkien's famous analysis of *Beowulf* called "The Monsters and the Critics." Tolkien begins the essay with an extended metaphor; it takes some time to find his thesis statement. I sometimes then show students, by way of contrast, another of the many scholarly articles on *Beowulf* that begin not just with an easily identifiable thesis statement, but possibly with a brief synopsis of the argument before the introduction. Not all students prefer one or the other, and that's okay; merit lies in discussion of the differences in approach.

- Look ahead to the sections on syntax in the next chapter for some ideas for revising introductions (and conclusions). Keep in mind an idea I discuss more fully in those sections: sometimes, sophisticated sentence structure demands that students express more sophisticated ideas. In other words, you can't write two sentences that are stylistically parallel unless you have first identified two linked ideas to discuss.

- Similarly, consider using the strategies in Chapter 4 of this book, "Getting It Together," with just the introductions of student essays. Peer groups, color coding, and other strategies can be applied to just the opening of an essay as effectively as with the whole piece. In particular, consider using metacognition (see Chapter 4 for a more in-depth discussion of this term)—have students write a brief reflection on the purpose and strategy behind every single sentence or phrase of an introduction. This approach would be tedious for a whole essay, but with just the opening paragraph it can serve to point out weaknesses and strengths quite clearly.

- Make sure the students revisit introductions *after* finishing a paper to be sure that their ideas remain consistent. It's not at all unusual to discover new facets of an argument while writing an essay, but students rarely go back and revise the opening of the paper accordingly. I've even used tricks like having students turn in the introduction on a separate sheet of paper from the rest of the essay, then handing back only the body paragraphs and conclusion and assigning the students to rewrite the introduction on the spot. Only when they're finished do I hand back the original opening and ask them to compare.

- Try giving students some room to explore. Tell them on one essay, for instance, that you want them to attempt, without fear of penalty, to start a piece in a manner they've never used before—with a joke, with a single sentence paragraph, with a metaphor. If the approach doesn't work, tell them so and initiate a discussion, but don't grade the work down.

- Save good samples to share with future classes. Save both original drafts and revisions; get the student's permission to use both, or remove names from the papers. Nothing works with students like accessible models.

BEYOND FIVE PARAGRAPHS: *Improving Organization*

To be a writer is to throw away a great deal, not to be satisfied, to type again, and then again and once more, and over and over.
—John Hersey

So far, I've asked you to consider how students can revise the openings of and overall ideas behind what they write. I've also tried to suggest that revision means moving beyond narrow structures for writing and toward more innate forms. I want to make this clear: structure has its place in learning to write; formulae can be useful; students need guidelines. But we're thinking about revision—about what can be done to help students express more mature ideas in more mature ways than the average essay may accomplish. The next stop on this path toward more professional writing is a organization.

So, ever been to McDonald's? Sure you have. Even vegetarians and health nuts end up in a McDonald's sooner or later—you can't avoid it. And for many of us, McDonald's is a comfort zone. You walk into any McDonald's from Alaska to Florida (or England, or China) and you know where you are—there's the counter, there's Ronald, there are the straws, there's the scary ball pit everyone tells me is a germ factory for kids, but that my daughters love. Everything in its place, just where you look for it.

Sort of like five-paragraph essays.

You'll never see a five-paragraph essay in the wild. You know the form, and by now, I hope, you envision it as one step on the way to better writing. Five paragraphs: an introduction where the thesis delineates three clear points, three body paragraphs supporting that thesis, and a conclusion that— well, honestly, most students don't really know *what* the conclusion is supposed to do, other than restate the thesis in words that are similar but not exactly the same. We'll get to that a bit later. In the meantime, I dare you to go look—take a trip to your local bookstore and scour the journals, periodicals, and books of literary criticism you find there. See if you can find a typical five-paragraph essay written by a professional author (samples of student papers don't count). You won't.

Spotting a five-paragraph essay in this setting would be like spotting McDonald's fries on the menu at a five-star restaurant. Or let's use a different metaphor: like seeing a skeleton doing its grocery shopping at your local supermarket. You'd recognize the structure right away, but it just wouldn't seem in place. Without the muscles, organs, skin, hair, and all of the other bits and pieces that make up a real person, the skeleton wouldn't seem real, unique, or even all that interesting—after the initial shock wore off. Imagine a store full of such skeletons shopping, and you can reproduce the way many English teachers feel when faced with grading a batch of standard five-paragraph snoozers. After a while, it's just the same old bones in the same old places, without a great deal to differentiate one set from another.

At this point, if you were one of my students, you'd ask the obvious question: *If English teachers get so bored reading five-paragraph essays, why do they teach us to write them? Why do they keep making these stupid assignments? And by the way, I like McDonald's.*

Yeah, but would you want to eat there every day for the rest of your life?

Think of it like this (and forgive me for stretching my metaphor): If you were going to teach someone to make a human being, where would you start? With the soul? With the fingernails? With the skin tones? Probably not—you'd probably need a skeleton first. But the skeleton by itself is just part of the overall product—just a piece of the picture.

Take this section of the chapter you're reading, for instance. You've made it to paragraph nine. We've covered two metaphors and included two one-sentence paragraphs. Granted, this isn't a piece of critical analysis with quoted evidence and examples, but the point remains. Real writing flows in an organic fashion, starting where it needs to start and ending when all has been said (or when as much has been said as is reasonable and appropriate). I could have begun the section with one of our now-familiar formulaic introductions, like this:

> Throughout history, mankind has analyzed literature and written down that analysis in an absolute number of paragraphs: five. Yet some authors claim that five paragraphs are not always the best number for writing an essay. By examining the content of an essay, the style of an essay, and the process of revision, it can be proven that not all essays need to be exactly five paragraphs long.

Instead, I tried something different.

Imagine reading thirty papers that start exactly like that paragraph (if you're a teacher, you won't have to imagine very hard). Imagine reading a hundred of them. Now imagine reading thousands of them, and you can get some feeling for what the scorers of AP exams, SAT writing sections, and standardized state writing examinations must feel like. Sometimes I can't quite imagine how those readers don't just bludgeon themselves with a stack of rubrics and get the whole thing over and done with quickly and easily.

But they, like teachers, are always thinking about the potential of that *next* paper, the one that's waiting for them in the stack. The one that makes literature come alive. The one with language that sings, or at least that speaks in a unique voice. The one that flows organically, basing its structure on what needs to be said rather than on how quickly the assignment needs to be finished, or on some idea that essays can only be written in one way.

They're waiting for that elusive essay that you just might find in the wild—the one with real muscles and flesh and personality, the one you can tell apart from all of the others, the one that feels *alive*.

Wow. That's a lot to ask of an essay.

True. But reading is too wonderful an activity to be so spoiled by the tedium of five paragraphs, just as food is too wonderful to be spoiled by the exact same menu every time you dine. Literature is too rich to be contained by over-simplified formats.

So we start with five paragraphs, okay. But then we revise.

Essay Organization

Keep this in mind: not every five-paragraph essay should follow the formula of a Five-Paragraph Essay. That's just one approach; the first step in revising an essay for organization is to ask whether or not the approach a student has chosen is the best strategy for the subject.

Consider an essay, for instance, on a poem most of us probably know well, "The Road Not Taken"—I certainly do, because a teacher named Ms. Higgins made me memorize it in middle school. I could proudly recite all four stanzas of the poem, but it was years before I actually paid much attention to what Frost actually wrote.

Here, for instance, is a planning chart made for an essay on the poem by a tenth-grade student, Bobby:

Section of Essay	Points/Examples	Analysis
Introduction	Thesis: By examining the choice the speaker is presented with, his thoughts about that choice, and his reflection upon that choice, one can see that it is truly better to have taken the metaphorical "road less traveled."	
Body Paragraph One	*The speaker's choice*	
	• Example one: "Two roads diverged in a yellow wood"	The roads are metaphorical—this is a life choice
	• Example two: "it was grassy and wanted wear"	One road is less traveled
Body Paragraph Two	*The speaker considers his choice*	
	• Example one: "Sorry I could not travel both"	He has to make a choice

	• Example two: "long I stood"	It's not an easy choice
	• Example three: "knowing how way leads on to way / I doubted if I should ever come back"	The choice will be final
Body Paragraph Three	*The speaker reflects upon his choice*	
	• Example one: "I shall be telling this with a sigh"	Speaker will be content with his choice
	• Example two: "I took the one less traveled by / And that has made all the difference"	Speaker made the right choice
Conclusion	The poem proves that it is better not to be a conformist.	

Ms. Higgins would have found Bobby's plan perfect, I suspect. And in Bobby's defense, he's doing exactly what he was taught to do: interpreting the poem in a five-paragraph essay with evidence and analysis. Assuming Bobby's grammar and syntax are up to the job, this will be a straightforward but proficient five-paragraph essay. Boring, but correct.

But there's another fly in the ointment, isn't there? Because *Bobby's interpretation is completely wrong.*

I'd make this argument: the structure doesn't challenge Bobby's thinking. In fact, it encourages him to pick out evidence that supports a narrow conclusion, and allows him to overlook, conveniently, any evidence that doesn't support his simple, three-part thesis. But if Bobby reconsiders his entire approach, he may be forced to reconsider.

What if, for instance, Bobby went another route, and wrote the essay in the standard Comparison and Contrast style assigned by many teachers? There are many versions of this approach; essays that compare and contrast two works or the similarities and differences between two characters, for instance, are probably the most common, but one might also write an essay that alternates between pros and cons, that presents a thesis (main idea), antithesis (counterargument), and synthesis (combination or logical resulting idea of the two). All of these variants point in generally the same direction—using contrast to strengthen an argument.

In this case, what two elements might Bobby compare?

Well, there are two roads . . .

Right. Two roads. Let's compare those. Bobby knows what he'll find—one road is less traveled, right? But he begins (with a sigh) by constructing a two-column chart as his teacher has instructed:

First Road	Second Road
bends in the undergrowth	as just as fair
	has perhaps the better claim
	grassy and wanted wear

So far, so good, though Bobby has a couple of mental questions he's hoping he won't have to confront, really. Why, for instance, is there undergrowth on the first road if it's less traveled? Is the undergrowth off in the forest? And why does the second road have the better claim "perhaps"? He's not certain? And why are they "as just as fair"? Even though one is less traveled, they're both pretty?

And then Bobby's ideas get derailed altogether, because in working systematically through the poem he's suddenly confronted with information about *both* roads: "Though as for that the passing there / Had worn them really about the same."

Wait a minute. They're the *same*? One was supposed to be less traveled!

And then: "both that morning equally lay / In leaves no step had trodden black." *Equally*? That doesn't fit into the chart. How can these roads be equal if the poem is called, as Bobby is sure it is, "The Road Less Traveled"? Then Bobby looks back at the title and sees that, in fact, it isn't titled that at all. Oops.

Bobby's thesis isn't looking so neat and simple anymore. The contrast isn't clear, so this form isn't really working out for him. At the same time, the five-paragraph form seems weak, because it clearly overlooks some really important lines.

So Bobby turns to a third structural model: explication. He works his way through the poem, from beginning to end. And even though his essay will still wind up including three body paragraphs, suddenly it's not a Five-Paragraph Essay, just an essay with five paragraphs and an acceptance of the poem's ambiguities:

Upon reflection, Bobby might well decide that, with so much evidence in his second body paragraph, he needs to break the middle section into two paragraphs. Suddenly he'll have six paragraphs exploring the poem with a logical "flow" and a more nuanced and sophisticated idea of what the poem says.

Section of Essay	Points/Examples	Analysis
Introduction/Thesis	Although the speaker suggests in the final stanza that he has taken the metaphorical "road less traveled" in his life, a close reading of the rest of the poem shows that his interpretation of his choice is not entirely accurate.	

Body Paragraph One: first stanza	The speaker has a choice to make—the specific choice is a metaphor for all choices.	
	• Example one: "Two roads diverged in a yellow wood"	The roads are metaphorical— this is a life choice
	• Example two: "it was grassy and wanted wear"	The speaker first presents one road as less traveled
Body Paragraph Two: second and third stanzas	The speaker's choice turns out to be a choice between two equal options.	
	• Example one: "bends in the undergrowth"	Road one may also be grown over
	• Example two: "as just as fair"	Suggests roads are equal
	• Example three: "perhaps"	Speaker is uncertain
	• Example four: "worn them really about the same"	It's becoming clearer that the roads are identical
	• Example five: "both that morning equally lay"	Now it's quite clear that they're identical
Body Paragraph Three: fourth stanza	In the final stanza, the speaker claims that he took the road less traveled by.	
	• Example one: "I shall be telling this with a sigh"	The sigh is ambiguous—is it a sigh of content, of regret?
	• Example two: dramatic pause ("And I—I took the one")	Why the pause? Is he trying to convince himself or us?
	• Example three: "I took the one less traveled by"	But the title of the poem is *not* "The Road Less Traveled," simply "The Road Not Taken"

continued

Section of Essay	Points/Examples	Analysis
Conclusion	The speaker clearly tries to present his choice differently later in life. The question is why: does he want to convince himself he made a bolder choice? Is he simply lying to us? Ultimately, the poem seems to be a comment on the way we remember our choices, not on the manner in which we make the choices themselves.	

That's what revision can do. To get there, I encourage students to take these steps:

- Consider multiple approaches to organizing your information. Might one yield a better interpretation of the work or issue?

- Go back to the evidence. If you haven't included evidence that doesn't entirely square with your thesis, you may not only need to revisit your thesis but also the way you've organized material.

- Go with your instincts. If you think there's a problem with the "flow" of information and the logic of your paper, don't just hope for the best. Try another approach and see if it feels better.

- Explain your organization, out loud, to someone else. See if it's the organization itself or the way you've written the information down that's giving you pause.

- Check your transitions. Transition words, phrases, and sentences are important to keep the logic of your argument clear.

- Check the ends of paragraphs. Be certain they tie back to ideas you've already presented.

- Make lists. Try listing details or ideas in columns and see if they square up the way you think they do. Sometimes a visual approach makes logic easier to follow and flaws in that logic easier to spot.

- Think of your essay as a map. Where does it start? Where does it end? Does it get somewhere or just go in circles? If it's just circular (i.e., it ends with a simple restatement of the thesis, nothing more), you may want to think about other approaches.

More Revision Strategies

No matter how often you talk to students about organic organization, voice, and moving beyond formulae, most will slip back into the structures with which they're familiar and comfortable. That's not a bad thing, for a first draft; revision is a time for improvement, however. The list that follows provides ideas for encouraging students to refine straightforward and formulaic essays—the five-paragraph sort included—so that organization becomes both more interesting and more natural.

- *Revisit the thesis.* Since I've already discussed this process fully, I won't belabor the point. But it works: as with a good essay, a good thesis is organic. A thesis that introduces complicated ideas will require careful and logical organization. Think about sentences: better sentences include subordination—so do essays. While the paragraphs should hang together and relate to the thesis, some paragraphs may include ideas that support other ideas in the paper. Some short paragraphs may exist solely as transitions from one idea to another. Some may summarize.

- *Give students a nudge in the right direction.* See what happens if you instruct them to include all or most of the following in a single revision:
  - A one-sentence paragraph
  - A paragraph that mainly asks questions
  - A list
  - A paragraph that uses one controlling metaphor to make a point
  - A paragraph that includes a relevant and appropriate joke

  Just possibly, such insertions will change not just the voice of the paper but also its underlying structure—in order for a controlling metaphor to make sense, the student might have to revise the number of paragraphs in the piece or the transitions between them.

- *Have students choose any paragraph from the essay for expansion.* Ask them to divide it in half. Then instruct them to develop each half into its own paragraph by exploring the idea more deeply and tying the idea to the thesis. This simple exercise can turn a five-paragraph essay into a six-paragraph essay and may necessitate revisiting the thesis statement itself—are there now nuances that need explanation, or are there simply four examples instead of three?

- *Have students rewrite a formal essay in another form.* I like to suggest an emailed letter to a grandparent, for instance. Allow them to use second person, fragments, slang, or any other elements of style, but emphasize that the point is to explain the issue as clearly as possible to dear old Grandma. When they're done, have them compare the organization of the letter to that of the original essay. Which makes more sense? Which is easier to understand? Can the two be combined to make a formal essay that flows more naturally?

- *Have students write out the essay as a set of instructions.* There are several approaches to this task that work; instructions can be given to the reader, a character, or the author, for instance. If a student has written about Othello's tragic flaw, have him or her write instructions to a reader who needs to find evidence of the flaw in the text, or instructions to Othello for overcoming the flaw as the play progresses, or instructions to an actor for making the flaw visible to an audience from the beginning of a performance to the end. Then reverse course and use the instructions to organize a formal paper.

- *Read and de-outline pieces—student samples or professional writing—that use complex or organic structure.* Earlier in the Chapter, I mentioned J. R. R. Tolkien's famous essay, "The Monsters and the Critics." It's a good piece because of its content, but the organization is even more interesting—the thesis statement, such as it is, is certainly not embedded in the first paragraph. Try using an article from a magazine like *The New Yorker* or *Harper's* for this exercise. Then talk about how students might apply such organic structure to their own work.

- *Spend some time in class discussing the difference between block structure and point-to-point structure.* Many times, either approach can be used to address the same prompt. Imagine an essay on rhetorical devices in Frost's poems, for instance. One essay might discuss all of the devices in "The Road Not Taken," then all of the devices in "Stopping by Woods on a Snowy Evening," and so on—this is block structure. A second essay might discuss similes in three poems, then alliteration in all poems, then other devices—this is point-to-point structure. Not only might either structure work better for different assignments, sometimes one structure makes more sense to one student or another and can offer a useful change of direction.

SOMETHING TO PROVE: *Incorporating Evidence*

> *I always have a quotation for everything—it saves original thinking.*
> —Dorothy L. Sayers

Here's what I think students are thinking when they write essays: "Gosh, I'd better include some quotations from the book so I don't fail."

Here's what I wish they were thinking: "I have a really good point here and I know this because there are quotations from the text to prove it; if I quote this material and then carefully examine and analyze the language, then I will have supported my thesis in the strongest possible way. It's important that I format my quoted material correctly so that the paper is easier to read; I'd also like to work the material into my sentences smoothly and clearly so that my paper will sound more sophisticated. And, of course, I want to cite my quotations correctly because it's important to give credit where credit is due and it's important for my reader to be able to find the material I quote easily."

Uh-huh.

Here's what my students are probably actually thinking: "I *hate* Mr. Gilmore."

The good news is that you can help students revise the use of evidence in their papers efficiently and with relative ease. It's not hard to figure out where evidence should be or to find where it already exists and improve the way it's incorporated. The bad news is that many students seem reluctant to have anything to do with evidence, especially specific evidence from a text or that involves research, in their essays. From the student's point of view, evidence is a pain—it takes time to find, it requires you to have completed some reading, and it has a pesky way of never saying quite what you want it to. From the teacher's point of view, any essay without quotations and specifics is unsupported, overly general, and has a weak argument.

So the first step in revision is often correcting for a lack of or even the *absence* of evidence, and that means not just forcing students to go out and find some random quotations but also teaching them *why* the evidence is important. Once they get it—that a paper without any support is about as useful as a sheet of math answers without the problems being solved—you can move on to revising the manner in which that evidence is incorporated into the paper.

Trials and Tribulations: Making the Case for Evidence

I intentionally use the word *argument* when referring to what a student has written rather than *content, topic,* or *subject matter*. I want students to think of their papers as arguments in the academic sense—works that take a stance and defend it. You think Tom Joad is just another murderer? Fine, prove it. You think Harry Potter is supposed to remind us of Christ? Show me the evidence. Argue your case.

And speaking of cases, the courtroom is an easy metaphor for why we write essays. Imagine the reaction if Johnnie Cochran, instead of issuing his now famous injunction to the jury ("If it [the glove] doesn't fit, you must acquit"), had just shrugged and said, "I've got this glove in my car with blood on it—it doesn't fit OJ. You'll just have to take my word for that because I can't be bothered to go get the glove right now." Imagine Atticus Finch standing in court and, rather than asking for testimonies, telling the judge, "Your honor, I just don't think Tom did it—I really, *really* don't."

Send students to any respected news magazine and they'll find examples of evidence pretty easily. Give them a sample that doesn't include any proof and contrast it with one that does and they'll immediately see the difference. Contrast, for instance, this sentence:

> The wealth of the United States is significantly different from that of the rest of the world.

With this one:

> At one American restaurant last New Year's eve, the price of a lobster gilded with twenty-four carat gold was forty-four dollars; a strangely popular item, considering that one-third of the world's population lives on less than two dollars per day.

Evidence works. It's not hard to convince students of this fact, though it seems strangely difficult to convince them that essays *don't* work *without* evidence. Put another way, students seem reluctant to put in the time it takes to collect adequate evidence for a paper. Here are a few techniques I've used to help them begin the process:

- Talk to students about the importance of marking a text during their first read. I encourage this practice in various ways—by making sure the students have texts to mark, first of all, or if that's impossible, by helping them come up with alternatives, such as a typed list of chapter titles, for instance, and space for notes with page references. I also allow students to use texts with notes in them for in-class essays and tests and model the practice myself—I often show students my own notes and chapter outlines in my texts.

- Use groups of students to collect evidence. Divide a text, for instance, between students, instructing each to find a number of relevant quotations from a certain section or chapter. Alternatively, assign individual students particular characters, scenes, or aspects of a topic and have them find quotations related to that aspect. Share the quotations and make them fair use for any students. It's an easy homework assignment. You can make the process fun by using wall posters when the students return to class—have students write their quotations on poster-sized paper hung around the room.

- Use online technology to find quotations. If there's an electronic version of the text available, as there is for many classic novels and plays, one can use the search function of an Internet browser or word processing program to find all of the times a particular word—*love* or *true love* or *death*, for instance—crop up.

- Students may roll their eyes, moan audibly, or mutiny and try to lock you in the supply closet, but one thing you can say about assigning them to create good, old-fashioned note cards with one piece of evidence on each one—you'll know they've done their research. This works with quotations from novels, secondary sources, interviews—all kinds of evidence.

- Make a game out of the process in class—who can most quickly find a quotation that reflects Macbeth's feelings of guilt? Put students in pairs and start lists on the board; they'll fill up quickly and the class will enjoy the activity at the same time.

Now You've Got It: Incorporating Quotations

Consider the use of quotations in this exerpt from a student paper:

> Not every reader is a fan of Jane Austen's style or subject matter, including Mark Twain. "Every time I read *Pride and Prejudice* I want to dig her up and beat her over the skull with her own shin-bone." Yet Austen herself defended her focus. "Three or four families in a country village is the very thing to work on."

You've got to love Twain, even if you also love Austen; he also quipped about Austen in one letter that it "seems a great pity that they allowed her to die a natural death."

Much as I enjoyed the quotations from these two authors, however, I'm not crazy about the way this student presented them. I call this method of throwing in evidence the "hanging quotation." There's no context, no indication of speaker or subject, no citation—it's entirely up to the reader to place such quotations in the argument.

The first fix for hanging quotations is so simple that it usually takes students twice as long to learn it (that's the way of simple lessons, I've found). The fix? Just give some context:

> As Mark Twain noted in an 1898 letter, "Every time I read . . ."

And so forth. It's better, but we can do better still. Look, for instance, at this paragraph from a paper comparing works by Orwell and Huxley:

> When the government in Huxley's *Brave New World* takes power after the Nine Years' War, it is "accompanied by a campaign against the Past; by the closing of museums, the blowing up of historical monuments;" the government obliterates all visual reminders of the past, since after all, if the people can not see it, they will not know to ask about it (Huxley 51). In addition, the government teaches that "history is bunk," which is why children are not taught the subject (Huxley 34). On the other hand, in *1984*, rather than banning and destroying

history, the Party rewrites it, not unlike political spinning, in order to preserve a history they want remembered. The Party "[alters], or, as the official phrase had it, [rectifies]," history, in order to "make the original figures . . . agree with the later ones" (Orwell 35–36).

—*Meg Gwatney*

Meg's early drafts looked much like every other student's. She included each quotation as its own sentence, followed by a sentence of analysis. The second sentence of this paragraph in one of her early papers would have read something like this:

On page thirty-four it says, "history is bunk." This quote shows that the government doesn't want history to be taught.

What Meg ultimately produced, however, was neither as stiff nor as predictable as this sentence. Though she may not have thought of it this way, Meg in fact learned during the course of a year to consider five steps every time she inserted evidence into her paper. Here are those five steps, along with tips you might offer students as you introduce them:

1. *Integration (working quotations smoothly into the text)*
   - Always work a quotation into a sentence of your own. A quotation must *never* serve as a sentence without some language you have written.
   - Consider working short phrases and words into your sentence rather than long chunks of text. They are easier to analyze.
   - Always maintain grammatical correctness where possible—in other words, make your sentence flow as smoothly as possible.

2. *Analysis (explaining quoted material)*
   - No matter what you're quoting, the author could have chosen different words to express it. Just ask yourself: Why did the author choose *these* words? How does that choice relate to your thesis? Then answer these questions within your sentence.

3. *Unity (choosing appropriate material to support an entire argument)*
   - If you can think of a point to make about a work, there's a quotation to back it up. You just have to find it.
   - Material you quote should come, when possible, from throughout a text—ask yourself if you've included *all* of the appropriate evidence, if your evidence really supports the points you're making, and if you've interspersed it throughout your paper evenly.

4. *Format (quoting material according to the rules)*

   • Keep commas and periods inside quotation marks.

   • If you're quoting one or two lines of poetry, incorporate them into your text and use a slash between lines.

   • If you're quoting a long passage, you can indent the passage. In this case, you place a colon after your introductory sentence, go to the next line, and indent. You do not use quotation marks.

   • You can alter the capitalization of the first letter of your quotation to make it fit your sentence.

   • You can use brackets to change a word or phrase, such as changing *him* to a proper name.

5. *Citation (identifying the source of the material)*

   • Citations go immediately after quoted material.

   • MLA format, used by most English teachers, is very simple: last word of sentence followed by parenthesis, author name, page number, parenthesis, period. There is no comma.

Much of this information is technical, but let's consider the first two steps: *integration* and *analysis*. Here's a simple revision strategy to help students make a smoother sentence when they've separated a quotation from its analysis:

   • Look at the material you plan to quote. Underline the most important words or phrases in the material—what is absolutely essential to make your point? Imagine, for instance, that you're writing a paper on the importance of money in *Pride and Prejudice* and that you want to include the first sentence: "It is a truth universally acknowledged that a single man in possession of a <u>good fortune</u> must be in want of a wife." Clearly the phrase *good fortune* is the most directly relevant to your case.

   • Write a sentence that fits into your paper using the underlined word or phrase. However, pretend that you're *not* quoting, that this is just a phrase you're using in a sentence summing up your topic:

   Clearly, the choice of a spouse in Austen's novel is usually determined as much by ~~money~~ good fortune as by romance.

   • Go back and put quotation marks around the evidence, and cite your source:

   Clearly, the choice of a spouse in Austen's novel is usually determined as much by "good fortune" as by romance (1).

- Ask yourself if you can use part of the rest of the quoted material in a similar way:

   Clearly, Austen's society usually expects "a single man" to attract a spouse based as much on "good fortune" as on romance (1).

But remember:

- Using this approach, one could easily quote in just about every sentence of a paper. It's important to remember the idea of *unity*: evidence should hold a paper together. One could, after all, quote like this:

   Clearly, Austen's society usually expects "a" husband to attract his "wife" based on his possession "of" money (1).

- Sometimes it's necessary to quote lengthy passages. In fact, it seems a shame not to include Austen's entire, perfectly worded sentence in this case. One can vary the way in which evidence is presented to great effect.

Almost no single improvement to an average student essay will make it sound more professional and mature than the smooth integration of quoted material; it's worth taking time to practice the skill with students. Try focusing one revision of a paper solely on the smooth incorporation of evidence and discuss the results with the class—you'll probably see the difference in every paper you assign from that point on.

More Ideas for Revising Evidence

Here are a few more strategies for helping students incorporate evidence into a paper:

- It's not always a bad idea to set a minimum amount of evidence for an essay, but such quotas have their drawbacks, as well. Many teachers I know insist on at least two quoted examples in each body paragraph of an essay (with analysis of each). The problem: students may find two examples and look no further, no matter how many relevant examples are available. Try asking, in revision, for students to double the number of quotations but shorten the length, making sure each is incorporated smoothly into a sentence.
- Try having students go back through a paper and list all of the quotations in columns: those that obviously agree with their thesis and those that do not. Very possibly, there won't be a single entry in the "do not agree"

column. Make them find some entries, if possible, and then incorporate them into the essay without weakening their thesis or conclusions. The best-case result is that students strengthen the argument by recognizing counterarguments and taking a stance against them; the worst-case scenario is that you have a discussion with students about why their essays fell apart when they inserted contradictory quotations, or why with a weak thesis one may not find contradictory evidence at all.

- With research papers and other essays that use secondary source material, revision is a good time to think about the legitimacy and accuracy of sources. It's also a good time to think about the variety and diversity of viewpoints.

- Have students go back through essays and take out all quotation marks. Make sure that all sentences read smoothly and that the grammar works. Then put quotation marks back in. (This one is easy with word processing programs; just use the find and replace function to remove and replace all quotation marks at once.)

ALL GOOD THINGS: *Revising Conclusions*

> *Great is the art of beginning, but greater is the art of ending.*
> —Henry Wadsworth Longfellow

A lot of novelists talk about how hard it is to end a work (E. M. Forster: "Ends always give me trouble"; Henry James: "The trouble is to leave off!"), but I've always suspected that poets and essayists have a harder time of it. After all, with fiction there are some obvious possibilities—kill everyone off or get them all married. It worked for Shakespeare.

How is a student supposed to end a personal or critical essay? I'm not sure most students (or teachers) are really certain, but I can suggest some *bad* ideas:

- Restate the thesis using just slightly different words.
- Add in a bunch of new information at the last minute.
- Include extraneous information just to fill up the space.
- Stay as vague as possible and hope your audience just stops reading.
- Write at the bottom of the last page: "Out of Time" (or any other excuse).
- Make a note to the reader: "See Introduction."

A weak conclusion is a problem presented by an overly simple thesis; if your thesis is quite simple to begin with, then there's really nothing to say in the conclusion. So what's the point in concluding at all? Why not just stop with paragraph four?

Conclusions can be powerful tools, that's why. They summarize, drive points home, and, ideally, leave a reader feeling satisfied and thoughtful. Here's a sample conclusion by Sarah, a high school junior, from an essay on the uses of propaganda in war:

> Perhaps truth is too complicated for war—not only for a war on terror, but any war. After all, war is always the ultimate simplification: the enemies are at the gate. Kill them. Subtleties and gray areas are obstacles on the path to victory. Unfortunately, no matter how worthy a nation's cause, those subtleties will always exist. Thus, even in a war of ideas—especially in a war of ideas—propaganda must exist. If correctly applied, it leaves no room for doubt, which is exactly what political leaders want.
>
> —*Sarah Brand*

It's tough to read a conclusion out of context, but you can see, at least, that Sarah doesn't fall victim to the worst mistakes students sometimes make; though she addresses her thesis, which includes the idea that propaganda necessarily "at once simplifies and distorts the issues surrounding war," she doesn't merely restate it, she expands upon it. Yet there's not any new information here—just a competent summary of ideas she's expressed and supported with evidence throughout the paper—but the paragraph does begin with a thought that could only come at the end of an argument, not at the beginning.

Now compare it to this conclusion, from a paper by another student in the same class:

> Since ancient times, propaganda has been a major tool of warfare. Even though some might consider their wars just and others do not, all use propaganda to sway people's thoughts. From Roman times on, propaganda has been a factor in public opinion.

The original thesis of this student's paper was that "leaders use propaganda to make the public believe that they need to fight a war." The conclusion, by the way, is the first time in the paper that ancient Rome is mentioned.

So, what conclusions can we draw from looking at conclusions about good approaches? First, here are two thoughts:

1. Not all concluding ideas are neat and tidy. Sometimes open-ended questions, suggestions, or possibilities are more useful than certainties in a conclusion, provided they are the logical result of a balanced discussion in the paper itself.

2. In a conclusion, syntax and wording matter. Sarah uses repetition, subordination, and short sentences to great effect (look at the sections on syntax in the next chapter of this book for more ideas; a good sentence can add drama to any ending).

Remember this, too: while introductions work more or less in the same way for any kind of essay, conclusions can have quite different jobs in different types of argument. An essay like Sarah's, which grapples with an abstract concept, must conclude by summarizing and hammering home ideas about an issue. An interpretation of a poem, on the other hand, has a different, though related, task: it must deal with the end of the work. We might add a third guideline:

3. In a paper that interprets a passage, novel, or poem, the conclusion of the essay should acknowledge the conclusion of the work—the shifts in meaning and idea that have taken place over the course of the text.

And a conclusion to a personal essay must approach the similar task of summarizing and satisfying the reader with a personal touch—not an easy trick to pull off.

A first step in revision might be to look back at a conclusion and ask if it's accomplishing anything at all. If it doesn't seem to serve a purpose, think about other common strategies writers use in conclusions—here are some general suggestions:

- Find another quotation or piece of evidence that's not new information but that summarizes your argument nicely. In a literary analysis, a quotation from the end of the piece (a novel's last line, for instance) can often serve to wrap up the argument.

- Pick up on an earlier point or idea, especially one from your introduction, and return to this idea. This works particularly well for personal essays or humorous pieces—take a look at essays by writers like Dave Barry or David Sedaris and you'll see this technique used often. Both ideas and syntax that are parallel to your introduction can be useful in closing the essay.

- In a persuasive essay, try applying the issue to universal or broader concerns. In some persuasive essays, a call to action might be appropriate. I'm not generally a fan of broadening the topic for essays that analyze literature, but a piece on, say, overpopulation in less developed countries might appropriately end with an exhortation for new policies and international programs. Likewise, some persuasive essays might include predictions in the conclusion.

- Break down the questions. The idea is not to bring up questions that you should have answered in the essay to begin with; rather, assuming that the argument has gray areas, divide them into questions or possibilities and recognize all before either taking a stand or discussing why the questions remain in balance with one another.

- Use a final metaphor. Sometimes an illustration can make a point vividly and succinctly.

It's worth remembering, too, that conclusions often rely as much on phrasing and how words are placed as they do on what is said. If the content is more or less established by the conclusion, it's worth the time to get the phrasing right. Though such ideas are covered more fully in the next chapter of this book, here are a few ideas that work particularly well in conclusions:

- *Parallel structure.* Somehow, with his neck in a noose and his true love headed back to England, Sidney Carton still had the presence of mind to use parallel structure, and we all remember that he's having a "far, far better rest" because of it.

- *A single short sentence at the end of the paragraph.* "Some may argue, like Smith, that it doesn't really matter whether or not we teach monkeys to crochet. The truth? It's absolutely vital."

- *A sentence that gains momentum and drama through a list.* "Holden rants, whines, complains, dreams, and wheedles his way into the heart of the reader through his constant appeals for us to `believe' what he's saying." Variations on this approach, such as asyndeton or a series of balanced pairs (see the next chapter for details), are also effective.

So, how to conclude a section on conclusions? First of all, with this thought: concluding well takes practice. Revision is important because almost no one gets the conclusion right the first time. Conclusions require a bag of tricks, or at least a bag with one trick in it (in the form of a syntactical structure or an approach to content) that a student can pull out again and again. Over time, students will find their own ways to spice up conclusions, if you give them the opportunity to practice and revise. Pull out conclusions, practice writing them in several different ways, peer edit the results, give students the chance to experiment and make mistakes, and somewhere down the line they'll begin to end their writing in that personal style that makes good endings work—by, well, drawing their own conclusions.

BETWEEN THE LINES: *Assessing Revision*

Grades are a double-edged sword. I've heard both criticisms and defenses of innumerable assessment systems, and I've only come to a couple of conclusions. One is that grades aren't going away, and another is that a grading system must be a contract between a teacher and students. It needn't be the same contract in every case, and it needn't be enforced in the same way, but the terms should be clear.

I'm also reasonably certain, however, that grades and the tools that accompany them—teacher comments, rubrics, penalties, extra credit, the weighting of assignments—all have the ability either to challenge students and help them learn or to do just the opposite, to intimidate and discourage students in such a way that they give up entirely.

In the introduction to this chapter, I suggested that revision should not take place only after a grade has been assigned and that not only students receiving poor grades be asked to revise. In addition to those thoughts, let me offer some others for your consideration as you plan to assess writing in your classroom:

- Not every assignment need be graded in the same way. Students will adjust as long as expectations and consequences are clearly laid out. With this in mind, you might try changing how you assess to reflect the skills you're teaching. Papers that will be revised might receive an all-or-nothing completion grade on a first draft and a more specific grade later on; in other cases, when students have been expected to revise *before* handing in the paper, a different grading system might apply.

- **Rubrics are only useful if they don't feel like a cage to students.** The student who doesn't really understand the vocabulary of the rubric may feel condemned to one little box—a three for syntax, a two for content. When students have a hand in generating rubrics, practice scoring sample papers using a rubric, or are presented with rubrics that offer general guidelines but not specific scores (rubrics, for instance, that remind students of the importance of a thesis or evidence without locking in a particular score for performance in these areas), these scoring guides can become useful points of discussion in themselves and may facilitate learning rather than inhibiting it. It's important, I think, to trust students—given the chance, they'll often help structure frameworks for their own learning happily. For more ideas about student-generated rubrics, see Chapter 4.

- **Progress in writing should be rewarded.** One problem with many grading systems and rubrics is that they don't allow teachers to reward attempts, only successes. Plenty of students may work hard to write a more organized and thoughtful paper, yet can't break past a single spot on a standard rubric. If we want to sell students on writing as a process, we need to find ways around these obstacles; teacher comments and other grading systems can help give students the boost in morale that improving writing occasionally requires.

continued

- Teachers have legitimate concerns about wanting to return compositions quickly and not overwhelm students with numerous areas of revision at once. Nonetheless, I believe that sometimes **we need to model the level of intellectual discourse about writing and analysis that we want our students to achieve.** This is especially true if we want students to review their overall concept and approach to what they write, and not simply "fix" the errors. Sometimes, I bite the bullet and type, say, a full page of comments in response to a three-page essay. I write such comments as letters; the purpose is to make the student feel that I'm a collaborator involved in a dialogue about the subject and the writing, not just a critic and scorekeeper. I can't do this with every paper a student writes, but I make a point of it occasionally.

- **Taking a stake in someone else's writing is an effective way of improving your own**. Students should be rewarded for editing and commenting on the work of others. Such rewards need not be tied to grades (though they could be) and need not be distributed unfairly; whole classes could benefit from extended deadlines or modifications to assignments. Because philosophies and systems of grading vary widely, I'm reluctant to prescribe any particular grading system for editing, but here are a few approaches I've seen teachers use with individual success:

  - Have students revise in pairs. Offer to add the number of points by which each student's paper improves to the original grade the partner received. In other words, a student's second draft grade might go up because of revisions she implemented herself; her first draft grade might go up, as well, because of revisions her partner made with her input.

  - Create a rubric with your students that evaluates peer comments. Allow students to suggest a grading scale and criteria for written comments on one another's papers, then use them to assess the editing process. Emphasize genuine attempts to be helpful; don't just reward students for "catching errors."

  - Use metacognition for editing—have students reflect on the process of editing one another's papers and their own. Give credit for the reflection and use it as a point of discussion.

As you consider strategies for student revision, be sure to balance your own need to handle the paper load (a valid concern) with the need of students for input that will lead to substantive review of their own writing. If you can keep yourself sane while returning comments or creating strategies that promote revision with more purpose than just improving a grade, you've pulled off a good trick—but it can be done. Students, I've found, take pride in improvement in their writing skills. They know writing is valuable and want to succeed as writers. What they need is encouragement and real opportunity to grow, and a focus on revision as part of the process and not as a penalty for poor writing is a solid first step toward giving students that support.

I WOULDN'T TRUST *WALDEN* FARTHER THAN I COULD THOREAU IT: *Interpreting Texts and Passages*

> *Books must be read as deliberately and reservedly as they are written.*
> —Henry David Thoreau

Back in high school, when I picked up *Walden* for the first time and realized there was a whole chapter called "Reading"—and that it was actually about *reading*—my heart sank; I didn't see many car chases, romantic scenes, or swordfights in my future with this one. I mean, this guy spent two years by himself in the woods measuring the thickness of ice. And I had to write an essay about it?

Walden cropped up again in college. A professor assigned yet another essay; but this time on only one short passage. I still recall the ending of that passage, in which Thoreau exhorts the community of Concord to aspire to greater standards of education:

> That is the *uncommon* school we want. Instead of noblemen, let us have noble villages of men. If it is necessary, omit one bridge over the river, go round a little there, and throw one arch at least over the darker gulf of ignorance which surrounds us.

I was stumped, I recall, by the professor's instructions simply to write an essay on the passage; no more than that. There was no particular question, no specific prompt that leant itself easily to three points. So instead I organized the piece in the most logical way I could—I wrote first about the beginning, then the middle, then the end of the passage. It worked, to an extent. The professor wrote back this comment: "You see this passage as a whole, not as a journey."

A journey? I was flummoxed. Thoreau never went *anywhere*.

I know, it's a metaphor. Once I figured that out, I figured out, too, a little bit more about interpreting passages of literature.

Preparing to Write Interpretive Papers

Because I teach (among other subjects) AP English, I spend a good deal of time with students planning approaches to interpretive essays, those that analyze a single passage, poem, or short piece of prose. There's an entire chapter of this book (Chapter 5) devoted to strategies for dealing with such essays when time is an issue, but it's worthwhile, first, to consider approaches to writing such essays without regard to time.

One might reasonably ask why we so often in the first place marry composition to literary analysis. It's worthwhile to discuss the close relationship we develop in English classes between books and essay writing—aren't reading and essay writing, in many ways, two separate skills? Need every composition be a piece of literary analysis? Shouldn't writing be a broader skill than that?

Sure. But at the same time, the reality of teaching middle or high school English includes teaching grammar, writing, reading skills, literary analysis, and a host of other skills with very little time. The result, in part, is that we often combine our focus; we teach students to write about the books we teach. We also teach how to write research papers, personal essays, creative writing, journaling, and more.

I'd argue, though, that close reading of a text, and especially close reading of a specific passage or poem, forces students to think about how they argue and how they write in a manner that actually encourages better writing and more thoughtful analysis in other arenas, as well. Students who learn to explore and catalogue the ambiguities of a sonnet become better thinkers in essays about politics, science, or history. So I think it's important, every now and then, to throw a passage at a student with the same simple instructions I got from that college professor: "Write an essay about this." It's also important to train students to handle such an assignment, not just because they may run into such prompts on an AP exam or in a college class, but because it requires them to collect and use logically a toolbox of analytical gear.

There are many ways of reading a passage in preparation for writing an essay. The method I offer here is simple and direct, and I've found it works. I can't include all of the circumstantial evidence, such as my own impressions of essays and student comprehension, but I can offer as evidence significant increases in AP scores of my own students who have worked through this method of reading and writing about short passages.

By way of introduction, let's imagine a sample prompt for the passage from *Walden* I mentioned previously; this prompt mirrors the kinds of questions generally asked on the AP English exam and similar tests:

> Read the passage below from *Walden*, paying particular attention to the concerns identified by the author and the solutions he suggests. Then, in a well-organized essay, discuss how Thoreau uses rhetoric to convince his readers that these solutions are viable and worthwhile. You may wish to pay attention to such rhetorical elements as tone, imagery, and syntax.

First, let's analyze the question. In this case, the question asks clearly for the student to write about rhetoric and how Thoreau uses it to convince us that his point of view is correct. The misleading part? That last sentence about "tone, imagery, and syntax," the section often called the *laundry list* by AP teachers (I don't know why we call it this; I've never made a list of my laundry and don't plan to, but I go with it). In fact, the AP prompts are including this sort of list less often, because students read it and immediately think they've been given a way to organize—a paragraph about tone, a paragraph about imagery, a paragraph about syntax.

The problem with that approach, other than that it may produce a formulaic essay, is that the student is likely to miss the most important points, the ideas. In fact, rhetorical tools are just that—tools. They're important, but only in the light of how the author uses them; rhetoric is not an end in itself. Instead, I back students up a bit and, after making sure they understand the question, suggest this approach:

- Break up the passage. If you can do this even before you read, all the better. There are clues: transition words such as *but* or *however* or *thus*, paragraph or stanza breaks, punctuation in poetry, noticeable changes of direction. In general, any short passage can probably be broken into two to four sections. Shakespeare's sonnets make for great practice at this approach—I literally have students draw horizontal lines between quatrains and notice how the rhyme scheme, punctuation, transition words, and syntax all suggest the same breaks in the poem. Take a look at Figure 2–2, which shows one student's notes on the middle of Sonnet 18.

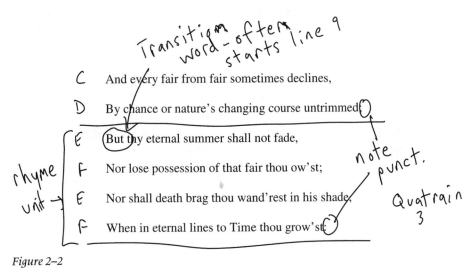

Figure 2–2

- Read, notate, and paraphrase the passage section by section. In particular, I ask students to look for *shifts* in meaning, points where the message or idea changes in some way—by adding contrasting ideas, by emphasizing an idea, by reinforcing meaning with new stylistic choices, and so forth. This is the key to understanding the "journey" of the passage. Think of it this way: if the passage is a selection of prose, as was the bit from *Walden* I encountered, some reader chose to begin and end the passage in a certain place; he or she could have included another paragraph, perhaps, at either end. Why not include it? Because there's some natural shift in meaning that's achieved by those specific paragraphs, some point that's been reached. The trick is to identify that point.

- Figure out the overall "meaning" or "meanings" of the piece—the main idea. Take into account the shifts that occur between sections. Then use that main idea to construct a thesis that also answers the question.

Note what's missing from this approach so far. I haven't yet even mentioned imagery, syntax, metaphors, diction, or the dozen other rhetorical strategies and hundreds of devices students might hone in on. A student who gets bogged down in the three examples of alliteration in a piece may well miss the big picture, the important ideas. The metaphor in the last line of Thoreau's chapter on reading is important, but not more important than the solution to a problem suggested by that line.

Moving on, however:

- Once you have the main idea and can use it to answer the question, construct your opening paragraph. Remember that you may revise this introduction after you've written more of the essay. This is just an opening.

- Write your way through the passage, logically leading up to the main idea by offering evidence from the passage from each section. Roughly, each section you identify becomes a paragraph (or more) of the essay. As you discuss the passage, look at the following for evidence *that supports the idea you're discussing*:

  - Rhetorical strategies: organization, tone, imagery, pacing, selection of details, irony
  - Rhetorical devices: simile, metaphor, alliteration, allusion, personification, onomatopoeia, hyperbole, and so forth
  - Stylistic choices: syntax, diction, point of view
  - Poetic elements: rhyme, meter, stanza length, form

What's important here is to emphasize, practice, and emphasize again (it takes a while for some students to get it) that discussing an author's rhetorical or stylistic choice is valuable *only if that discussion reinforces the discussion about meaning*. Recognizing an example of alliteration is fine. Identifying it in a paper is useless unless the alliteration has a purpose. What does it accomplish? Why is it there?

Take Thoreau's last line:

> If it is necessary, omit one bridge over the river, go round a little there, and throw one arch at least over the darker gulf of ignorance which surrounds us.

The metaphor is obvious. But *why* is it important? Do bridges have some particular context for Thoreau's audience? Is a bridge a particularly good metaphor for getting past ignorance—better than, say, a metaphor of digging into knowledge, or of building a house, or of singing, or of a hundred other actions one could use in this way? Probably so—the metaphor here draws a fine connection between the literal and symbolic worlds and offers a visible symbol of rising above an abyss. A bit of exploration of the metaphor, in fact, helps the writer reinforce Thoreau's point, while simply identifying the device would serve little purpose at all. Likewise, the turn of phrase in the penultimate sentence—converting "noblemen" to "noble villages of men"—uses rhythm, expectation, and repetition to drive home the contrast between nobility of class and nobility of spirit; only discussion of the turn of phrase, not just identification of it as a rhetorical element, can further understanding of the entire piece.

That's it, the whole approach. Not every essay will be successful—students will misinterpret passages, misunderstand words, miss elements altogether—but more often than not, a student who focuses on big ideas first and devices and tools second will produce a solid analytical piece. And then it's time to revise.

Revising Interpretive Essays

The previous reading and writing process works equally well for revision. Let's say, for instance, that a student didn't follow the process in a first draft. Imagine a thesis statement in response to the prompt that reads like this:

> Through his clever creation of a caustic tone, elaborate syntax, and rich imagery, Thoreau persuades his reader that ignorance is more costly than material conveniences.

It's not a misreading of the passage, but we can tell by now what's coming, right? Three paragraphs on tone, syntax, and imagery. The student de-emphasizes the importance of Thoreau's purpose, however, and may lose sight of it altogether in the essay itself. The body paragraph on syntax may include several examples but may neglect to tie that device to the overall point about ignorance. Worse yet, the student may entirely miss some very important aspects of Thoreau's writing that have nothing to do with tone, syntax, or imagery.

Directing this student through the revision process with the following instructions might help:

- Make sure you've connected the overall meaning of the passage or poem to the question. Have you, in every paragraph, reinforced your interpretation of the writer's overall idea or meaning? Have you, in every paragraph, provided part of an answer to the substantive aspects of the prompt?

- Make sure you've covered the entire passage and included evidence. Have you quoted from the beginning, middle, and end of the passage? Have you included all evidence that is obviously a key part of the argument or idea of the writer? (This is especially important for essays that cover only a few aspects of rhetoric—it's easy to miss lines or passages that *don't* serve as excellent examples of one of those areas but are of key significance overall.)

- Look more deeply at rhetorical, stylistic, and poetic choices. Search through the passage or poem for examples of choices the writer made. For each, try to determine the reason behind the choice—if you can't, you may not want to mention the device or strategy at all. If you can, discuss the choice in such a way that it bolsters your overall interpretation.

- Look closely at the ending of the selection. What point has been reached that is different from the opening of the selection? What is the journey of the passage? Use this last point or idea, and any shifts that precede it, to drive home your interpretation in your last body paragraph and conclusion.

- Remember to take the title of the piece into account. If it sheds any light on the piece that is not obvious until the end of the passage, be sure to include it in your discussion of the overall point of the passage by the end of your essay.

Years after first encountering *Walden* in high school, I was asked to teach it to a class of juniors studying American Literature. I recall pulling down my old, battered copy of the text from college and thinking to myself that the copious notes I remembered writing during my professor's lectures would surely be of benefit, only to find that all I'd really written were a few obvious and fairly basic comments in the margins—nothing of much substance, and certainly nothing that would help determine how I'd teach the work overall.

What that volume did help with was the identification of some passages I'd found interesting or important in that college class. Rereading those passages led me to reread others, and eventually I turned back and read the entire work again. Thoreau was quite a prose stylist—he could turn a phrase, construct a metaphor, and devise a sentence with great care. There were still no car chases or romantic encounters, but there were elements that drew me in nonetheless. None of those stylistic elements, however, were more important than the content of Thoreau's discussion. He went to the woods "to live deliberately." I want students to write, and to read, and to *revise*, with the same sense of deliberation and intent.

3 *Awk! Frag!*

Revising Style

I remember the first time I realized that I had adopted a foreign language as my own—not French, nor Spanish, but that strange tongue of abbreviated and cryptic marginal scrawls known only to English teachers. "Awk," I had written in the margin of a student's essay (written about what Hamlet thinks it means "to be") again and again. Unfortunately, in my haste to comment and return the paper, the final "k" tended to look like a letter "f." The student—let's call him, oh, René Descarte—handed in the revision a week later with a sheepish look.

"I hope you don't think this one is awful, too," René said.

I wanted to explain, but as I thought about it, I wondered how much difference there was, really, between the way I'd "commented" on the paper and the effect of just writing the word "awful" at the top. After all, I'd barely mentioned anything positive—my "comments" were largely an intimidating, peripheral sea of marks indicating mistakes: AWK! FRAG! SP! In some places, I'd just put question marks: ? ? ?

I understood what they meant. Other English teachers probably would, too. But poor René might as well have been looking at a page of hieroglyphics.

One lesson was immediately clear: if I wanted students to revise, or even just to proofread, effectively, I'd have to be both clearer and more expansive in my responses to their work. But another lesson struck me, as well: René couldn't revise effectively because I hadn't taught him *what* to revise. All I'd given him was the chance to "fix" the "problems" in his paper. Sure, I'd written some general comments at the top of the essay, but how was he to apply those comments to an entire essay if he didn't have the first clue what tools and resources he had at his disposal?

Let's assume that René's ideas were not, in fact, awful, that the content of his work was strong but the execution sometimes flawed—in fact, this student was quite a good writer, so the assumption is valid. Let's say he had constructed a solid thesis and written a fairly decent paper despite a few awkward spots.

Remember the revision cone (Figure 2–1)? René, having determined the content of his paper and structuring the argument well, could now narrow his focus.

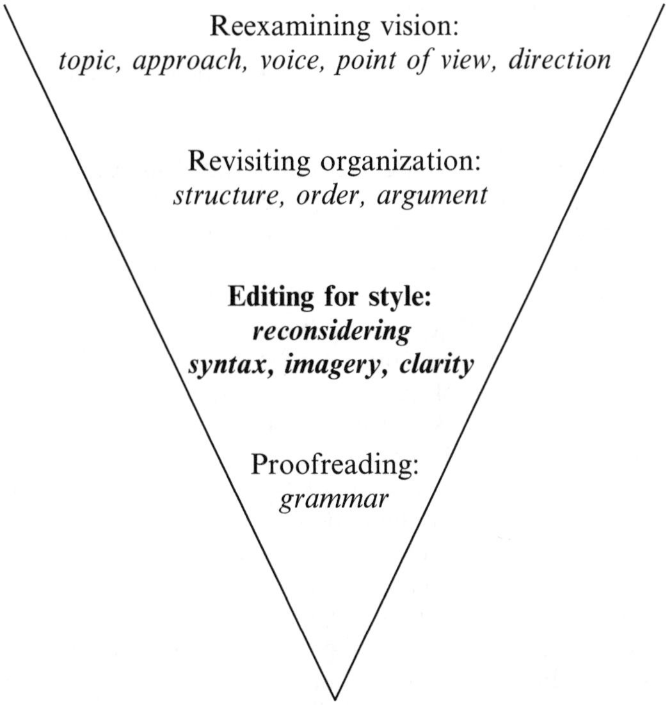

Reexamining vision:
topic, approach, voice, point of view, direction

Revisiting organization:
structure, order, argument

Editing for style:
reconsidering
syntax, imagery, clarity

Proofreading:
grammar

Figure 3–1

If the argument weren't strong, of course, we'd begin revision at the top of the cone (so as not to, as the old joke goes, put Descartes before the horse), but René was ready to move past the broadest reconsideration of his subject matter to a more specific (but not unimportant) aspect of his writing—his style (see Figure 3–1). The remainder of this chapter focuses on the aspects of that style, including clarity, syntax, diction, and voice, that could help a student like René create a paper that would receive more than just "awked" or "fragged" notes and more than just marginal scribbles, that would not provoke responses in the foreign language of English teachers but that would communicate and sing with a language of its own.

I NEVER METAPHOR I DIDN'T LIKE: *Finding What Works*

> *Art comes out of art; it begins with imitation.*
> —Alan Bennett

Imagine this: your in-laws are coming over for dinner. You've promised them you'll cook their favorite dish—say, oh, shrimp bouillabaisse. The problem?

You have no idea how to *spell* bouillabaisse, much less cook one. Your kitchen is fully stocked, the table is set, you have all of the tools you need, and you have an afternoon free, but you don't have a clue how to make the actual dish. So what do you do?

Call Pizza Hut?

Well, maybe, but it's not going to result in the elegant repast you'd hoped to serve. But you do have other options, places to turn for help. You can look at a recipe. Call your mom. Turn on the Food Network and hope for the best.

In short, you look for models. Someone else, you reason, must have done this before. Someone else has come up with just the right mix of ingredients, a formula—or at least a set of guidelines. If there's an expert, a professional, or just someone experienced, then you can imitate, emulate, learn.

Writing's no different, of course. A high school senior faced with the prospect of writing a college essay faces a level of stress at least equal to, and possibly far greater than, that of the erstwhile chef in my fictional example above. It happens all the time: a student has the tools, the time, and the topic—perhaps he or she even feels pretty confident about writing in a general sense—but no one's ever prepared him or her for *this* task, *this* particular dish.

Oh, we may think we prepare our students. I've been guilty of this one more than once. I make the assignment, suggest a number of pages, talk about the topic with my class, perhaps even give a few pointers. Be specific in your college essay, I tell them. Make sure the reader gets to know you. Avoid proselytizing or recounting your last basketball game play by play.

Then I throw the class to the wolves, thinking I've done my job. The actual writing is up to them; I can't write anything for them, can I?

No, I can't. But I can offer models, and here's the key: I can help them learn from those models. I can help them figure out what works, as long as it's a good enough model with style that *does* work.

Take the writing of Mary Beth Epps, for instance. Never heard of her? I'm not surprised, unless you were in my AP English class last year. Mary Beth was a good student and a solid writer. Was she a budding James Joyce? Not really, but who'd want to read *his* college essay, anyway?

In the fall of her senior year, Mary Beth wrote—and revised—her college essay. The following two paragraphs are just an excerpt:

> It was the playbill that won the first tack in the cork board; "The Phantom of the Opera" inspired me not only to seek out the ones refused compassion from the world, but also to learn the ways of the theatre, to desire to create the next Don Juan who would bring the ghosts of people's hearts up from the basements to the center stage. Then, rolling across the board, a time-stream of pictures: friends, family, boys, better times. The one my eyes always find amidst the multitude is of a young girl and a handsome boy, his arms wrapped around her with a smile and glowing face, the same tack pinning down a ticket to a concert, a first date, a first kiss.

The simple words, the simple pieces of paper, the simple incidents that make a person; how can someone put into words the colorfulness of the mind and soul without showing the cork board, filled with not only thousands of tacks, but empty holes, from papers taken out and never replaced? Try reading between the lines of immature love letters, asking what happened at the birthday parties, concerts and movies after reading the invitations and tickets, studying the expressions of faces in the dozens of pictures, attending the various conventions commemorated by nametags, laughing at all the cheap bumper-stickers with mind-provoking sayings, or crying on the drawings from appreciative camp children. Here before me, staring me in the face at every break and eve, is all the inspiration I need to fit together the puzzle of my life: just a smaller piece of the puzzle I will find myself connected to when my new cork board is being filled on the first day of college.

It's not bad, is it? The students in my next class thought it was pretty good—and, unlike their attitudes about reading James Joyce, they thought to themselves, *Hey, I could do that.* Mary Beth's writing is a good model because it's accessible, it's familiar, and it works.

The question is *why* does it work?

Let's begin with the obvious: Mary Beth doesn't simply describe the items on a bulletin board, she consciously uses her writing to describe these items in a way that makes the bulletin board representative of her personality, her interests—in short, of her.

Look: what's the point of the essay, anyway?

To help us get to know Mary Beth. And to prove that she can put together a few sentences with style.

Right. There are ten thousand people applying for admission to a college, and something in this essay has to make Mary Beth stand out—the essay has to help us get to know her. It also has to be well-written, but fortunately those two tasks go hand in hand. So, what do we know about Mary Beth?

She experienced her first kiss at a concert. She works at a summer camp. She likes musicals. She views her life as a puzzle.

Ah, a real puzzle? She's a bunch of jigsaw pieces?

Of course not. She's using a metaphor.

And there it is, easy as that: we've identified a metaphor. When you start looking, in fact, metaphors are all over the place. If you don't believe me, go back and read the first paragraph of this chapter again.

Students don't have much trouble figuring out what works in an essay if you give them a chance. The questions and answers here aren't all that unlikely to occur in a real classroom, and then, bingo, you've got a list of Things That Work in an Essay: detail and a metaphor. The next step: do it yourself.

Hold that thought—we'll get to the DIY exercises in the rest of this chapter. First, let's think a little more carefully about our new category (Things That Work in an Essay) and how to fill it up even more.

Modeling What Works

The first step for engaging students in a discussion about revision possibilities is choosing a model. Just tell yourself you've got it easier than the art teacher down the hall; at least you don't have trouble getting your models to stay still. Really, anything works—a sample from a former student, a piece you've written yourself, an article from the newspaper, a paragraph of *Huck Finn*. As long as the piece demonstrates good writing and represents the style or genre your students are working with, any model will do. I prefer to mix things up, to show students models of various types throughout the year.

So, you choose a model. What's next? It's pretty simple, I think:

1. Mark what works.
2. Share and discuss.

Let's take these steps one at a time.

Marking What Works

I've seen this done in a number of ways, but the simplest is probably the best: have students circle or underline whatever they like as someone in the class reads the passage aloud. With a more advanced class, you could be more specific—have them mark specific rhetorical devices or syntactical structures—but you probably don't need to; students tend to circle the good stuff in good writing.

You can also, if you wish, give students other, slightly more specific instructions. Colors might be used to mark various aspects of writing (rhetorical devices, syntax, diction, even individual parts of speech); if you have access to the technology, most word processing programs, including Microsoft Word, have a highlighting function that might serve the same purpose. You might have students annotate their choices with explanations of what, precisely, is effective about the author's choices. You might have them pick out the two best sentences, the best verbs, or the two most striking images, and explain in the margin, at least briefly, why those examples stuck out.

And there's another take on this method, too, but one I caution you to use carefully: you can have students mark those aspects of the piece that specifically *don't* work. Why the caution? For one thing, it's not always a good idea, with samples written by students, to point out the flaws publicly—even if the author is not in the class. Negativity breeds itself; students might take the chance to criticize as an opportunity to be cruel (perhaps without meaning to be), cynical, or self-aggrandizing. That's not to say we should never recognize flaws in writing, but I wouldn't be too anxious to let the search for weaknesses outweigh the positive benefits of learning from what others do well.

Sharing and Discussion

Again, the simple approach to sharing those lines or phrases that students think work, works: just ask, "What did you mark?"

But, you say, *the same two kids always answer my question.*

Ah. How about this?

- Have students share and compare their marked passages in pairs, then ask the pairs to share with the entire class only those passages that both partners marked.

- Have one student read the passage aloud. As he or she reads, all other students signal the words or phrases they marked by raising a hand or even reading those words and phrases aloud in unison with the main reader.

- Make wall posters by hanging several big sheets of paper around the room. Label each one with a category: syntax, diction, rhetorical devices, punctuation, etc. Each student should write a word or two (or you could number sentences in the sample passage for easy reference) to identify the passages they thought worked. When everyone has listed at least one item on each poster, lead the discussion by taking one sheet of big paper at a time and comparing what's listed there.

No matter what method you use to share, remember that sharing is only the start. This is a great opportunity to discuss not just what works, but *why.* There are two steps to this process: one is naming the devices writers use, and the next is figuring out, all names aside, why we should care.

Take the sample from Mary Beth's college essay we discussed earlier. When I shared this sample with my class, the conversation went something like this:

ME: Homer, I noticed you raised your hand to signal that you'd underlined the end of the first sentence.

HOMER: Yeah, I like that metaphor about bringing the ghosts of people's hearts from the basement to center stage.

ME: Good; I'm glad you noticed it's a metaphor. Why do you think it works?

HOMER: Um . . . I'm not so good with metaphors.

VERGIL: I think it works because it constructs the image out of the actual content of the story it's talking about—it isn't just a random metaphor, it actually builds on what came before it.

ME: Good point. Thanks, Vergil. Homer, what else did you mark?

HOMER: I really like those two lists—I think they're sort of the same. The one that says "friends, family, boys, better times," and also that one at the end of the paragraph: "a concert, a first date, a first kiss."

ME: Okay, why those?

HOMER: It's cool how there aren't any conjunctions in them.

ME: Technically, that's called asyndeton. Why do you think it works?

HOMER: It builds up this rhythm. Oh, and since the last thing in the list is kind of abstract, it sort of hammers that home.

ME: Good point. Vergil, do you agree?

VERGIL: About the asyndeton?

ME: Right.

VERGIL (shrugging): Hey, it's all Greek to me.

Keep examining Mary Beth's essay and you'll find the repetition for effect that begins the second paragraph, the rhetorical question, the nice use of colons. Homer might have pointed out, too, the use of alliteration in the phrase, "friends, family, boys, better times." Good models are rich with good examples, and while the opportunity to label those good examples for ease of communication about rhetoric is useful in the classroom, the opportunity to discuss *why* good writing works is invaluable.

Some students, of course, are going to try to get off easy. "I just like how it sounds," they'll say. Or, "I like that sentence because I can picture it." There's nothing wrong with either of these statements, except that they don't really delve deeply into language. *Why* is the sound pleasing? *Why* can we picture the scene? There's always an answer, if the reader is patient enough—and for the writer, the answer to these questions means the difference between writing and writing well.

And it's not just rhetorical devices that you'll want to discuss with students. AP readers talk about the "laundry list" of rhetorical aspects that students should be able to identify and discuss: diction, syntax, imagery, pacing, organization, tone, and irony, just for starters. You can point out that closed syntax or a compound-complex sentence in much the same way you point out a simile.

But keep this in mind, too: just as most students have a larger vocabulary for reading than they do for writing, so, too, most recognize more sentence types or rhetorical strategies when they read than they can or will effectively employ in their own writing. This is where practice, preparation, and revision come in—a good rough draft can turn into a shining second draft *if* a student has some ideas about what to add, alter, or rearrange.

Think of it this way: as a guest, I don't need to worry too much about why I like shrimp bouillabaisse. I can just eat it and enjoy. Unless I want to cook it myself. Or I want to order something similar. Or I want to devise a menu to complement the dish. Or I want to discuss possible variations with my in-laws. Then I need some comprehension of the ingredients, the process, the recipe—some idea of what works, and how, and why.

BETWEEN THE LINES: *Roll Out the Barrels*

There are monkeys in my classroom. No kidding: a whole chain of those little plastic monkeys—red ones—that come in toy barrels; they're hanging from a light fixture. A student named Alex hung them there after I tried to use a metaphor about barrels in class; I let the metaphor slip out of my control, grow out of proportion, and then floundered helplessly as it became its own monster with teeth and sharp little claws and—well, you get the idea. By the end of the period, the students were laughing at my desperate attempts to rein in my own imagery. But they remembered the point.

The point was this: a writer needs resources at his or her disposal. Gathering these resources takes time and experience, but the process can be deliberately helped along. Imagine, I told the students, that you're sitting at your desk, composing a piece of writing, surrounded by barrels. One of them has every rhetorical device you know in it, one has marks of punctuation, one has syntactical models. Some of the barrels are fully stocked, others have very little inside—your goal is to fill them up with accessible, ready-to-hand materials, like a barrel full of monkeys.

Monkeys?

In class, this is where things got silly. Nonetheless, sure: monkeys. You know how they interlock their little plastic arms to make a chain? It works for writing resources, too. You can't do much with just one monkey, one type of sentence, one rhetorical device. But start to build up the supply and soon you can pepper a piece of writing with a variety of sentences, asyndeton here and chiasmus there, and a chain begins to form.

Throughout this chapter, you'll find examples of these barrels. In the first barrel, for instance, you'll find a list of rhetorical devices I encourage students to learn and use. This is not the same list of devices I expect student to recognize in their reading—it's less comprehensive and more practical. Similes and onomatopoeia, for instance, don't make the cut on my list because students tend either to use them naturally or, if they construct them deliberately, run the risk of sounding elementary. There's no synecdoche on the list because, let's face it, you're not likely to see a unique synecdoche included on purpose (a student may write "All hands on deck" in a story, but he or she probably isn't thinking about synecdoche).

The terms in the list that follows are those I've found that students will learn, remember, and effectively apply to drafts in the revision process. To prove my point, the first example of each device in the list is not a famous quotation or saying that exemplifies the device (though those are easy to find), but an example that comes from an actual student paper on *Romeo and Juliet*; all of the examples are by students who added the devices to their own barrels and now use them consistently and well—with no, um, monkey business.

Barrel 1: Rhetorical Devices Students Can—and Will—Actually Use

Why these devices?

There are literally hundreds of rhetorical devices students could learn. Many teachers expect students to recognize a large number of them when they read; this list is intended not for readers but for aspiring writers. Why these ten? Partly because they:

- are easy to remember and reproduce;
- add drama and flair to student writing without sounding unnatural or forced;
- can be used consistently in most types of writing and for most assignments;
- actually force students to think in more complex terms—to take a simple idea and expand or build upon it in some way.

Again, it isn't necessary to know the names of the terms in order to remember and use them—focus on the effect, not the term.

1. **Allusion** (reference to person, event, or work of art in an external context)
   - Romeo and Juliet, like Pyramus and Thisbe, suffer an unhappy love affair because of the injustice of their parents' expectations.
   - My English teacher, like Brutus, stabbed me in the back with that grade.

2. **Anadiplosis** (repetition of a word or phrase at the end of one clause and the beginning of the next—clauses are often arranged in order of increasing importance)
   - The nurse loves Juliet, Juliet loves Romeo, and Romeo mainly loves the idea of being in love.
   - The students frustrate the teachers, the teachers frustrate the administrators, and the administrators frustrate everyone.

3. **Anaphora** (repetition of a word or phrase at the start of successive clauses)
   - Romeo loves Juliet, Romeo loves Mercutio, but Romeo loves love itself most of all.
   - I have to write an essay, I have to do a science report, I have to do my math homework—I have to get some sleep.

4. **Antithesis** (the juxtaposition of contrasting words or ideas)

   - Romeo wrongly kills, but he does it for the right reasons.

   - My homework was eight pages long, but the teacher's response included only four letters.

5. **Asyndeton** (a phrase in which conjunctions are purposefully left out)

   - Mercutio fights, Mercutio laughs, Mercutio dies—he does all three for Romeo's sake.

   - I came, I saw, I went home sick.

6. **Chiasmus** (reversal of terms from one phrase in a second, parallel phrase)

   - Juliet suffers an undeserved death for the right reasons; Tybalt suffers a deserved death for the wrong reasons.

   - Absences resulted in his failing grades, but his failing grades resulted in more absences.

7. **Ellipsis** (the purposeful omission of a word or phrase from a sentence)

   - Romeo loves Juliet; Juliet, Romeo.

   - Some students earn their grades; others, their reputations.

8. **Metaphor** (a comparison of one thing to another)

   - Romeo is a puppy in the balcony scene and a wolf when Mercutio is killed.

   - That math teacher is a dinosaur—she's been here a million years.

9. **Polysyndeton** (a phrase using many conjunctions—the opposite of asyndeton)

   - Juliet is young and beautiful and idealistic and destined for unhappiness.

   - I worked and worked and worked and failed.

10. **Tricolon** (three or more words or phrases of the same length within a sentence)

    - Romeo loves hard, fights poorly, and dies young.

    - I carried my books to school, my backpack to class, and my disappointment home.

SYDNEY CARTON LOST HIS MIND OVER A GIRL: *Clarity*

> *Have something to say, and say it as clearly as you can. That is the only secret of style.*
>
> —Matthew Arnold

Words are tricksters—and combinations of words are even worse. Just ask the student whose mother wrote me this note on the morning he showed up without his homework: *Please excuse John's missing essay for illness. He managed to start the paper several times before he finally threw up.* I knew the kid was sick of writing assignments, but I didn't realize *how* sick.

Or this example: the school principal I once heard address a graduating class with the words, "I'd like you to know that you're *exactly* the kind of students we want leaving our school."

Clarity matters. Why? For one thing, clarity can help you avoid unintentional double entendres, such as those just cited, that can make you seem foolish (the title of this section comes from an essay on *A Tale of Two Cities*—the last sentence: "Carton dies by guillotine for Lucie Manette, the girl he lost his mind over"). But it's not only the obvious twists of meaning that students need to learn to avoid; they also need to strive for clear communication. Take this sentence from an essay by an actual student (but for the sake of discussion, let's pretend our friend young Will Shakespeare wrote it):

> Each character in *A Midsummer Night's Dream* is significantly different in their own way not only because of their social class but also because of their various morals and additionally through whether or not they are of the male or female gender.

Reading a sentence like Will's is always a little bit like I imagine chewing dog food would feel: you know there's nutritional stuff in there, but it's still hard to swallow. What, after all, does the sentence really say?

The characters' differences stem from discrepancies in social class, morality, and gender.

So what's getting in the way of saying that more easily? What does this student need in order to express this thought clearly?

1. Precise diction

2. Economy of language

3. Grammatically correct syntax

There you have it: the recipe for clarity. Be specific, be concise, be correct, but also make your syntax and vocabulary interesting. It can be tougher than it sounds, especially because we sometimes send contradictory signals to students. I've actually had this conversation in class any number of times:

ME: Will, why say "of the male and female gender" instead of just "male or female"?

WILL: I just thought it sounded, you know, more essay-ish.

ME: Does the sentence sound natural to you?

WILL: No, but you always say we shouldn't write in the same voice we use when we talk.

ME: Sure; you don't want to sound like a text message, like when you wrote "2B or not 2B, what wuz the ?" That doesn't mean you have to sound stiff—you want the sentence to flow naturally. Why don't you just tell me what you were trying to say here?

WILL: I was saying that the characters are different overall because they're different in class, sex, and, um, morality.

ME: Let's start with that sentence in your draft; then we'll see about sprucing it up, okay? In fact, how about, "they differ in class, gender, and morals."

WILL: Really? I can just say "morals"? I thought that needed more, you know, words and stuff.

ME: I think it's fine.

WILL (muttering as he leaves): Lord, what fools these morals be . . .

It's true; I tell classes that the voices they create for formal writing, conversation, and emails to friends might not require the same rules—mostly because I tire of reading sentences about what "would of" happened or that describe Hamlet as "chillin' with Horatio." If the natural result is unnecessary complication, then a first step in revision must be to alleviate that complication, to improve clarity.

Revision Strategies

Here, again, are our goals:

1. Precise diction
2. Economy of language
3. Grammatically correct syntax

We'll take them on one at a time.

1. *Having the Last Word* (diction)

There's so often a better, more precise word for what we write in first drafts. *Tree* can be replaced by *oak* or *willow*, *newspaper* by *Wall Street Journal*, *run* by *sprint* or *dash*, *mean* by *calloused*. Sending students to a thesaurus can be dangerous, of course; it's easy to wind up either with words being misused ("Why can't I say that my mom *mitigated* the butter? The dictionary defined it as meaning *softened*.") or with fifty-cent words all over the place—an example of the lack of economy, which we discuss next. Still, more specific diction often results in more specific denotation and better communication. In creative writing, it means the difference between a good line and a great one—in expository writing, it means the difference between clarity and confusion.

The examples that follow include some common scofflaws of student essays—errors to watch for in any revision exercise.

Diction—Worst Offenders

- **Thing**

> Ralph looks for ways to improve things on the island, while Jack looks for things to amuse the boys.

Unless we're talking about the characters from *The Cat in the Hat*, there's almost always a better, more specific noun than "thing." In this sentence, any number of words would improve either clause. For example, Ralph might want to improve conditions, the situation, his lifestyle, their chances of survival, the decision-making system; as originally written, however, the first clause could easily mean that Ralph doesn't think the island is quite up to par and wants to put in a pool and patio.

- **It** (referring to an entire work or narrator)

> In chapter twenty-three, it says that Grendel's mother wants revenge.

We'll deal with the rest of this sentence in a moment; let's just think about the word *it* for a moment. What is *it*? The novel? The narrator (or speaker)? A character? A passage? One answer is to condense the whole line: "Chapter twenty-three suggests that Grendel's mother wants revenge."

- **Says**

> In chapter twenty-three, it says that Grendel's mother wants revenge.

Later in this chapter, you'll find a longer discussion of the word *says*. Amateur writers often use this word as a catch-all to refer to the function of a novel, a scene, a quotation, or even an idea. Remind students not only that novels or passages don't speak, but also that if, in fact, a passage "says" something, you ought to be able to quote it.

- **This, that** (indefinite pronouns)

  This is the meaning of the poem and it was symbolic of what happened in his other poems, as well.

A friend of mine recently sent me this example. My response: huh?

- **He and she** (pronoun reference issues)

  Dickens describes Pip's encounter with Magwitch in the graveyard and he points out his fear of the situation.

Dickens (or is it Magwitch?), apparently, is afraid of his own scenes.

- **Adverbs** (especially to create unnecessary hyperbole)

  Faulkner writes incredibly long sentences in order to make the characters seem very confused.

There's no need for either of these adverbs.

- **Noun forms that invite heavy syntax** (-tion, -sion, -ment)

  It is John Proctor's assertion that he wishes his wife, Elizabeth, to live in contentment.

Can't Proctor simply "assert" that he wants his wife to "be content"?

2. *An Engfish Education* (economy)

Engfish is the term coined by Ken Macrorie to describe the kind of convoluted syntax in Will's sentence about *A Midsummer's Night Dream*. The word, taken from an anecdotal student's writing, is meant to describe "the phony, pretentious language of the schools" (Macrorie, *Searching Writing*, 22). There's a fine line to walk between English and Engfish—we want students to write well, to write formally, and to write with an authentic voice, all of which sometimes translates in the student's head to "write like a student."

The result: more words than necessary, bigger words than necessary, and convoluted references to characters who are "significantly different in their own way" instead of just "different." Even in personal writing—journals, poems, reflections—students often adopt a fake, "academic" tone rather than a natural, organic voice. How does one combat Engfish? Through revision, through discussion of voice and writing, through practice. And, too, one can focus on economy in language, which not only means using fewer words but also thinking about the clearest way to phrase a thought. You might try these strategies:

- Once a first draft is complete, lower the word count for a second draft—force students to cut, say, ten words from each paragraph without cutting the number of sentences, or to cut one hundred words from an entire draft.

- Have students underline or highlight any *phrase* in the first draft—a combination of words that can't be separated. Then consider shorter possibilities for each phrase in the paper; not all need be replaced, but some probably could.

- Instruct students to read first drafts aloud (see Chapter 4 for detailed ideas about this approach) in order to hear forced language.

In economizing language, there are a few worst offenders to watch for:

Economy—Worst Offenders

- due to the fact that (*since, because*)
- despite the fact that (*although*)
- it is stated by the author that (*the author says*)
- this is the reason why (*this is why, because*)
- the text of the book (*the text*)

Also, in the interest of precision and economy, you might have students excise overly generic and hyperbolic terms from essays:

- Writers use similes in order to . . .
- Many readers feel that . . .
- It has often been stated that . . .
- It is important to note that . . .

3. *Serving the Full Sentence* (*grammatical syntax*)

There are two entire sections of this chapter that include ideas for helping students to improve syntax. For now, let's focus on a few of the most obvious ways in which students use syntax to mangle sense in their sentences.

Syntax—Worst Offenders

- **Is when**

> The best example of Elizabeth's independence in *Pride and Prejudice* is when she walks through the rain to see her sick sister.

Combined with a failure to use literary present tense, this construction might become "was when." Students might also separate the construction: "is the moment in the novel when . . ." The trick here is to change the subject: "Elizabeth demonstrates her independence when she walks through the rain."

- **Ambiguous references** (especially using *which* in a subordinate clause)

> Macbeth kills his enemies and tries to kill their families, which makes him more evil.

Before committing the error in this sentence, some students will try to make subordinate clauses beginning with *which* into separate sentences: "I wrote this sentence in my paper. Which is why I might fail." There's also the common confusion over *which*, *that*, and *who* to confront. But it's the indeterminate reference in the sample sentence that I see otherwise confident writers fall back on too often. Another example of a common ambiguous reference: "Sir Thomas More wanted the king to change his mind, but he couldn't decide what to do."

- **Dangling and misplaced modifiers**

> Displaying feminine charm and allure, Macbeth finds Lady Macbeth's arguments convincing.

I call this one the English teacher's favorite, because if nothing else, it's amusing. One of my favorites, from a paper on *Grapes of Wrath*: "While killing a man, Tom's mother was making the family dinner."

- **Subject-verb incongruities**

> Many reasons can be found that question whether the characters are truly in love.

Students often embue reasons, attitudes, ideas, attributes, and other abstract aspects of a work with the ability to question or prove a point.

In Conclusion: Revising for Clarity

The problem with developing general strategies for revising work for clarity is the nature of student writing itself—although there are some common obstacles students face in writing, clearly every student creates his or her own obstacles as well. There's no catch-all rubric that will ensure clear, focused writing.

So how do we help students to achieve our goals of writing precisely, economically, and correctly, yet with interesting style? Here are a few thoughts:

- Reading good models will help students appreciate the effects of clear style.
- It may be worthwhile to have students practice clarifying convoluted and awkward sentences to get them thinking about clarity, but such exercises are probably not enough to ensure that students then write clearly.

- Reading aloud and peer revision strategies (see Chapter 4 for detailed ideas) will help students identify and correct unclear writing.

- Practicing reduction of sentences, paragraphs, and entire compositions is a good way for writers to focus on clarity.

The next sections, which discuss diction and syntax in more depth, may also be useful as techniques for encouraging clear thinking and writing.

IN THE MOOD: *Improving Verbs and Adjectives*

> *They've a temper, some of them—particularly verbs: they're the proudest—adjectives you can do anything with, but not verbs— however, I can manage the whole lot of them!*
>
> —Lewis Carroll

Now that you're familiar with the concept of barrels, there are two barrels vital for any process of revision that I insist every student in my classes works to fill (yes, yes, I know—now we're going after monkeys with both barrels). The two barrels? Verbs. Adjectives. And, specifically, the verbs and adjectives that get used, over-used, and abused in student essays—those skulking culprits of the trite and banal. If nouns are the bricks from which sentences are built, I tell students, then verbs are the bricklayers who help construct sentences; adjectives are the painters.

Take a look at this sample from a student essay, again from an essay on *A Tale of Two Cities*—we'll call the author Charlie:

> Dickens uses many examples of symbols to allow the reader to grasp the entire tone of the novel. He says, "Footsteps not easily cleaned again if stained red." He uses the crowd's footsteps stained red to symbolize death; the footsteps are red because they are bloody. In this way, tone is used to make the reader feel the danger in the society.

Certainly, there are some issues of clarity and syntax in Charlie's writing. There are also key opportunities to turn this paragraph into a strong analysis. Look at the strategies that follow to see what I mean.

The Bricklayers—Revising Verbs

Step 1: Identify Weak Verbs

To begin with, let's list all of the main verbs in Charlie's paragraph:

uses	are
says	is used (again, but this time in passive voice)
uses (again)	

It's not a particularly exciting list, but not an uncommon one, either. The worst offenders fall into two fairly simple categories:

Generic Verbs	Verbs That Express Authorial Intent
To be (is, are)	To use (the author uses . . .)
To have (has)	To say (the author says . . .)
To do (does)	To state (the author states . . .)

A student probably won't manage to write any piece without a few of the generic verbs from the first list; probably, no student should try to. It's necessary to include these verbs, but it's not necessary to include them in every sentence.

Step 2: Substitute Better Verbs

Often, there's simply a better, more commanding verb available:

> *The footsteps are red because they are bloody.*

> Blood turns the footsteps red.

> Or:

> The footsteps gleam red with blood.

> Or, combining this sentence with the next:

> The bloody footsteps impart a sense of lurking danger.

In these examples, the verb imparts clarity to the sentence.

Step 3: Make Passive Verbs Active

Passive voice, too, tends to rob verbs of their power. Charlie writes, "In this way, tone is used to make readers feel the danger." Making the verb active empowers the sentence by giving it a specific agent: "Dickens uses tone . . ."

Step 4: Find Better Verbs for Authorial Intent. Here we revisit verbs such as *use* and *say* and look at two possible approaches to revision. The first is simply to employ some more specific cousins of these words:

> *He uses the crowd's footsteps stained red*

> The author . . .

> employs, utilizes

> *He says, "Footsteps . . ."*

The author . . .

asserts, states, notes, describes, suggests, contends, exemplifies, presents, demonstrates, etc.

So far, so good. At least this list provides Charlie with some variety for the introduction of quotations, rhetorical devices, or details.

But what if Charlie took the process one step further? What if he looked into his barrel of verbs and found some far, far better places to go with the sentences? We might take a second approach and end up with a paragraph like this:

Dickens furnishes his story with symbols in order to generate the tone of *A Tale of Two Cities*. The author peppers the story with images such as "footsteps not easily cleaned again if stained red" and, in so doing, evokes an atmosphere of danger and death.

Strong verbs propel sentences *and* enhance content. The barrel that follows offers more verbs students can use in place of *use*.

A final note about verbs: *says* and *use* are worst offenders, but other banal verbs have a tendency to sneak into student papers repeatedly. The verb *gets*, for instance, shows up in many sentences: "Finally, Atticus gets Scout to wear a dress." Any number of more interesting verbs (*commands, wheedles, entices*) are available. Other common verbs to watch for are *has, does,* and *puts* (as in this gem from a student paper: "Shakespeare doesn't put much modern language into his plays, but then, neither does any other author who's been dead a really long time").

Barrel 2: Verbs to Describe Authorial Intent

This barrel is not a comprehensive list of replacements for the verbs in phrases such as "the author uses" or "the author says." Rather, these words are merely representative of a vast number of possibilities.

The author . . .

advises	coaxes	educates	extracts	initiates
amasses	confers	effects change	fashions	instructs
assembles	constructs	embraces	frames	intertwines
batters	crafts	endows	fuels	intones
buffets	creates	engenders	furnishes	kindles
catalogs	croons	entwines	generates	knits
celebrates	details	epitomizes	highlights	molds
chisels out	devises	equips	hints	paints
coats	dusts	etches	ignites	peppers

plaits	provokes	realizes	roots out	validates
populates	pummels	records	salvages	weaves
profiles	rallies	renders	sprinkles	whittles

The Painters—Revising Adjectives

Chekhov (the Russian writer, I have to remind students, not the navigator from *Star Trek*), famously said, "When you read proof, take out adjectives and adverbs wherever you can." He wouldn't have liked, for instance, the word *famously* in the last sentence. So much for him.

Actually, it's not bad advice for a novelist or poet. Adverbs, in particular, tend to serve in place of strong verbs or dialogue—why note that a character said something "slyly" if you can connote the slyness through what's actually said? Adjectives, too, get strung together by amateur writers who seem worried that one won't cut it, but is a dog who is "big, black, and mean" more fearsome than a "snarling Doberman"?

For students, there are times when adjectives are not only useful but vital. In particular, students need modifiers to describe tone, mood, voice, attitude, style, atmosphere, and meaning.

Again, Charlie's first sentence:

Dickens uses many examples of symbols to allow the reader to grasp the entire tone of the novel *A Tale of Two Cities*.

We rewrote it like this:

Dickens furnishes his story with symbols in order to generate the tone of *A Tale of Two Cities*.

It's better, but still not satisfying. Crucial to the development of this sentence is some specification of the tone under discussion; without that information, the sentence goes nowhere. The sentence attempts to answer a *how* question, but neglects to offer a full explanation of *why*.

So, what tone do the symbols create? Charlie almost gets there in his last sentence: the reader can "feel the danger in the society," he tells us, and we revised this to describe "an atmosphere of danger and death." So, the atmosphere, or mood, perhaps, is one of danger. What tone creates a sense of danger?

An ominous one?

Right.

Threatening, maybe? Portentous? Menacing?

That's it; keep using that thesaurus.

Any of these words would add accuracy to a general statement; now, Dickens furnishes the novel with *portents* that create an *ominous* tone. I know exactly what to expect—images of blood, gloom, foreboding. Bloody footsteps and guillotines, perhaps. If you want some more ideas for adjectives that work with the word *tone*, check out Barrel 3.

As I said, so much for Chekhov. We'll keep the adjectives.

But, as one clever student pointed out, Chekhov *had* to cut stuff out because, after all, he was *Russian*—the rest of us can take our own sweet time.

Barrel 3: Adjectives to Modify Tone, Mood, Attitude, or Style

As a classroom exercise, I sometimes give my students only the base adjectives on the left (or others like them) and have them search out synonyms. Be careful that this list does not provoke overwritten work—just a couple of good adjectives are enough to win over an audience. You might, in fact, discuss with students whether or not some of these words are actually synonyms at all—that discussion alone might help to improve the precision with which students choose adjectives.

afraid	trepidatious, disquieted, frightened, timorous, apprehensive
angry	irritated, aggravated, irked, vexed, nettled, piqued, irascible, caustic, peevish, corrosive, petulant, shrewish, contentious, belligerent, infuriated, querulous
astonished	wondering, rapt, marveling, dumbfounded, awed, stupefied
bold	brazen, impudent, impertinent, insolent, shameless, flippant, audacious
casual	informal, unpretentious, affable, familiar, unceremonious, plain, unaffected, unassuming
eager	impatient, anxious, zestful, vivacious, heated, passionate, intent, breathless, frenetic, avid, frenzied, feverish, hysterical, ardent, fervent, vehement, impassioned, zealous
formal	pedantic, legalistic, sacerdotal, extrinsic, ceremonious, stately, punctilious, meticulous, precise
happy	euphoric, gratified, titillating, joyful, blissful, elated, jubilant, jovial, delighted, ecstatic, contented, radiant, rapturous, enchanted, exultant, blithe, exhilarated, genial, sanguine, optimistic, breezy
indifferent	cold, cool, perfunctory, unenthusiastic, disinterested, insouciant, nonchalant, numb, apathetic, lackadaisical, halfhearted, tepid, neutral, vapid, detached
kind	benevolent, philanthropic, gracious, warmhearted, altruistic, amiable
nostalgic	sentimental, reflective, regretful, remorseful, contrite, penitent, maudlin, wistful, pining
sad	joyless, displeased, disquieted, anguished, vexed, chagrined, distressed, afflicted, tormented, agonized, dejected, despondent, languishing, melancholic, bleak, morose, sullen, disconsolate
serious	solemn, sober, grave, staid, sedate, formal, earnest

unfeeling	callous, insensitive, coarse, brutal, obdurate
unkind	malicious, malevolent, unamiable, rancorous, virulent, acidic, acerbic, caustic, noxious, vitriolic, incisive, biting, scathing, astringent, callous
witty	humorous, whimsical, ludicrous, eccentric, quaint, farcical, incongruous, jocular, facetious, sarcastic, satirical, ironic, droll, playful, bantering

THE WAGES OF SYNTAX: *Fashioning Better Sentences . . .*

> *A sentence is both the opportunity and the limit of thought—what we have to think with, and what we have to think in.*
> — Wendell Berry

Sophisticated sentences lead to sophisticated thinking. That's such an important point, I'm going to repeat it: **sophisticated sentences lead to sophisticated thinking**. Learning that one lesson can help students improve introductions, conclusions, thesis statements . . . well, everything, really.

Here's what I mean. This sentence comes from the first draft of a student essay on *The Grapes of Wrath*:

> The Joads travel from Oklahoma to California and its agricultural belt, but they seem to encounter more despair as they see wealth around them.

That sentence does the trick. It includes a nice juxtaposition of the characters' feelings with their surroundings. It's not bad. Now look at the revision:

> From Oklahoma to California, from the center of the dust bowl to the center of an agricultural belt, from strength despite poverty to despair amidst great wealth, the Joads cling to one another as they travel.

A bit weighty, perhaps, but now we don't just see the juxtaposition of the feelings and the surroundings, we have a sense that the state of the characters' feelings, like the plot itself, involves a journey of contrasts; we also see the importance of community and family as a part of the journey.

The difference between the second version of the sentence and the first is that the student wasn't just writing down her thoughts in the revision in whatever manner she thought of first; she used a sentence *form*, one she'd learned and practiced. In much the same way that students need to learn essay forms like the five-paragraph or comparison-contrast structures, forms they may grow beyond after mastering, they also need to learn sentence forms. They may grow beyond such forms eventually and craft sentences that are both sophisticated and organic, but the process of learning must take place.

It's a two-step process. First, students must learn to review and revise some of the simplest elements of their sentences and how they use them: length, variety, and basic structure. Then, they can focus on advanced forms of syntax.

Three Strategies for Revising Syntax

1. Length

Before I ask students to rewrite sentences, I want them to reexamine the sentences they've written. An obvious, though imperfect, gauge of sentence sophistication is length, so I have students count the number of words in every sentence of an essay. Then I ask them to assign each sentence they've written a label: short (ten words or fewer), medium (between ten and twenty words), or long (over twenty words). This paragraph, for instance, contains two medium and two long sentences.

The first point of discussion, generally, is the nature of the labels themselves. The numbers are obviously arbitrary—I've seen other sources that call anything under fourteen words short, for instance. Students sometimes think that an eighteen-word sentence is quite long, while for others it's an average length. (You could have students calculate the average length of sentences in an essay—this is especially easy on a word processor, where one can look at the exact word count and divide by the number of sentences).

Once your students have the numbers—the words per sentence, the average sentence length—discussion and revision can begin. Some points you may wish to make:

- The goal is *not* to write all long sentences. In fact, most sentences in an essay should probably fall in the range of fifteen to twenty words. A few shorter or longer sentences, if well-placed, can offer emphasis and variety.

- Clumps of long or short sentences should probably be reexamined. Short sentences can be combined and longer sentences broken up.

- There are some natural spots for longer sentences—a thesis statement, for instance, sometimes requires more room. One also shouldn't worry too much if a quotation makes a sentence long, though long quotations within the text (rather than set off by indentation) can be distracting.

- If every sentence in an essay is around fourteen or fifteen words in length, the rhythm of the piece as a whole may suffer. Even within the ranges of short, medium, and long sentences, variety is desirable.

2. Sentence Variety

A simple strategy for examining the variety of sentence structure in a paper begins with making a list of the first four or five words in every sentence and then looking for patterns:

First Four Words	Notes
Dickens uses the symbol of	Subject-verb
However, he also uses	Transition word followed by subject-verb
Tellson's Bank is a	Subject-verb
This shows that the	Subject-verb
Another example occurs in	Subject-verb

This chart represents the sentence from one paragraph of a student essay. Clearly, the student is mired in a single type of construction and could stand to revise by adding, for instance, a subordinate clause at the beginning of a sentence. Here is the original third sentence from this paragraph:

> Tellson's Bank is a dark, dismal, and traditional enterprise that reminds the reader of a prison.

The sentence works (it's not great, but it works) but could also be modified to provide variety within the paragraph:

- A dark, dismal, and traditional enterprise, Tellson's bank reminds the reader of a prison.

- Reminding the reader of a prison, Tellson's Bank is dark, dismal, and traditional.

- Tellson's Bank, which reminds the reader of a prison, is dark, dismal, and traditional.

Personally, I'd choose the first revision.

Revision for sentence variety requires a knowledge of subordination and some fluency with sentence structure. To help students with this skill, I'd suggest using peer editing groups and having students write samples on the board to revise as a class.

3. Sentence Combining

Sentence combining is no new exercise—in fact, it's a fairly common practice in many language arts classrooms. It helps to vary sentence structure and length and also teaches students to examine the artistry and choices involved in syntax. The most common exercise involves deconstructing a long sentence into short statements (or just creating several short statements) and having students reconstruct a single sentence. Take, for instance, this list:

1. Ernest Vincent Wright was a novelist.

2. He wrote a novel called *Gadsby*.

3. The novel *Gadsby* should not be confused with *The Great Gatsby*.

4. F. Scott Fitzgerald wrote *The Great Gatsby*.

5. *Gadsby* does not contain a single letter E.

All true, by the way. These five sentences might be combined into one like this:

> Ernest Vincent Wright's novel *Gadsby*, which does not contain a single letter E, should not be confused with the *The Great Gatsby* by F. Scott Fitzgerald.

The more initial sentences one begins with, the greater the need for careful subordination and punctuation. Sentence combining is not only good practice for students considering syntax, it can also help with the appreciation of an author's style. Some teachers deconstruct sentences from works they're teaching and have students reconstruct them as an entry point to a discussion about the work's particular strengths. I wouldn't try it with William Faulkner or James Joyce, but it works with most other writers.

For the purposes of revision, try using sentence combining with student compositions in some of the following ways:

- Identify any clusters of short sentences in a student composition. Have the student try sentence combining to find possibilities for revision.

- If a student has trouble with writing particularly long sentences, try reversing the process—have the student break the sentence down into pieces, then come up with two or three ways of recombining those pieces. Sometimes two stronger medium-length sentences will emerge.

- Use sentence combining when a class is creating thesis statements. Have students work together to list all of the nuances, questions, or possible lines of discussion a topic might raise, then combine elements from those lists to create a more sophisticated thesis.

- Use sentence combining to create parallel sentences. Break a long sentence into its smallest elements, then work to make the elements parallel. When they are recombined, keep the parallel structure intact. Sometimes this step-by-step approach helps students understand the nature of a parallel sentence better. In my sentence combining example, for instance, there are some obvious possibilities for parallelisms: two sentences identify the authors of novels, so the entire sentence could have been written: "Ernest Vincent Wright's novel *Gadsby* contains no letter E; F. Scott Fitzgerald's *The Great Gatsby* contains one in the title."

Before Moving Forward: A Note About Complicating Synta

Some students will naturally gravitate toward more complicated syntax, and some may even begin to discover, particularly if they read great writing, advanced sentence forms. That's great, but it also raises a flag for teachers. As we transition from thinking about making sentences longer and more complex to styling sophisticated sentence forms (the topic of the next section), it's worth considering the shaky ground I'm leading you onto.

Sentences that exist for their own sake can impoverish a piece of writing in the same way that too many vocabulary words can ruin a perfectly good thought. Authors have, for ages, railed against amateur writers who overwrite, who try too hard to impose "style" on their prose. The exercises in this section and the next may encourage students to do just that—at first. But remember, school is where we learn, and one must learn to write before unlearning, like an architect who studies cathedrals before building the perfect, simple doghouse. I encourage you to allow students to flex a little literary muscle before reining them in, to try some extravagance before deciding where extravagance is appropriate and where it isn't. Eventually, the best writers will refine their own styles with an awareness that balances what's possible with what's appropriate.

GETTING CRAFTY: . . . *And Even Better Sentences*

> *If you never write sentences longer than twenty words, you'll be like a pianist who uses only the middle octave: you can carry the tune, but without much variety or range.*
>
> —Joseph Williams

Ever heard this one?

"You have to learn the rules before you're allowed to break them."

It's a fairly common defense that English teachers use when students complain that the books they read break grammar rules all the time—professional writers use sentence fragments, split infinitives, oddly placed commas, and make up words seemingly at will. And it's true; much of the time, good writers break rules intentionally, knowing full well why they're doing so.

Still, how often do we hear the instruction that should, at some point, logically follow this restriction?

"Hey, everyone; now it's time to start breaking the rules. Have at it."

Of course, it's not all about breaking rules, though most writers would agree that a well-placed sentence fragment can be useful. Powerful, even.

As can, say, the one-sentence paragraph that draws attention to itself and punctuates an important concept.

Or the intentional colloquialism that just sounds better, as Winston Churchill illustrated with his famous rejoinder to the grammar hound who called him on ending a sentence with a preposition: "This is the sort of English up with which I will not put."

Of course, sophisticated and grammatically *correct* sentence forms must be combined with such intentional breaches of the rules to create a style that sounds at once natural and intentional. Finding the right balance can be a trick; it comes with practice. But first, students must learn the forms with which to experiment.

Even though English is fairly picky, as languages go, about the order in which words appear in a sentence, there are still hundreds of ways to combine elements within many sentences. Sentence combining, which I described in the previous section, helps students recognize this fact, but learning some specific, more sophisticated forms may give students a goal in sentence combining and formation. To this end, I like to present students who are ready for such forms with a small number of options, to populate a barrel of syntax with a few well-chosen possibilities.

Take a look at the structures in the barrel that follows. It's probably not a good idea to present them all to students at once; I introduce such sentence forms gradually throughout a course. In particular, if we come across such a form in our reading, I'll often stop, discuss the syntax of the example, and then have students try it out on their own. In the section that follows Barrel 4, you'll find a discussion of some possible revision strategies—other ways to get students to try to remember the forms and to use them wisely.

Barrel 4: Advanced Sentence Forms

To some extent, the first barrel in this chapter—the barrel of rhetorical devices—demands syntactical structures as well. Many of those devices can be combined with these advanced forms easily.

Again, I recommend introducing these forms one at a time and warning students against loading up papers or stories with such structures; they're meant to create a dramatic effect and to promote more sophisticated analysis and reasoning, not to be ends in and of themselves. The examples for each sentence type are taken from analytical papers on commonly taught pieces of literature.

Form 1: An idea set off by a colon or dash

- The character of Ma in Steinbeck's *Grapes of Wrath* lives by a single rule: keep the family together.

- *Heart of Darkness* presents us with the contrasting worlds of Europe and Africa so that we may ultimately see the common trait they share: savagery.

Form 2: A series of three balanced pairs

- The most famous lovers of English literature—Romeo and Juliet, Lancelot and Guinevere, Antony and Cleopatra—all had to overcome obstacles to their love in order to be together.

The first (revised) sample sentence of the section, "The Wages of Syntax," is an example of a series of three balanced pairs as well, and it ends with an abstract pairing (see p. 77). It's a particularly effective strategy, as is building drama within the pairs themselves, as this example demonstrates:

- Shakespeare's *Hamlet* is a story of murder and revenge, of crime and punishment, but most of all of love and the consequences of love.

Form 3: A "not only this, but that" construction

This form forces the writer to make a comparison of some sort:

- Shakespeare's *A Midsummer Night's Dream* teaches the reader that most lovers are not only fickle, but often blithely unaware of the reasons for their love.
- *The Mayor of Casterbridge* is not only a story of regret, but also a story about the need to forgive.

Form 4: A dependent clause starting with "that" as a subject

This form can easily sound contrived, but it can sometimes be particularly effective for first or last lines of essays. Punctuation is key with this form, and distinguishes it from a sentence such as this one: "That Wilde play, the one over there, is mine."

- That the American Dream proved to be as much a burden as a guide to happiness is clear to anyone who reads Arthur Miller's *Death of a Salesman*.
- That Wilde's play involves the ridiculous is clear from a first reading, but deeper analysis shows that the ridiculous often betrays a serious aspect of society: hypocrisy.

Form 5: Repetition of a key (and important) word

- *The Book of Job* presents a story about suffering—and about redemption through that suffering.
- Ultimately, there is no idea more important in *Heart of Darkness* than the savagery that exists in every human being, savagery that cannot be hidden no matter how civilized a society seems.

Form 6: Using a semicolon to create a more or less parallel sentence (two independent clauses)

- Macbeth is driven to a horrible act of violence by his wife; Lady Macbeth is driven to such an act by her own naked ambition.
- Holden Caulfield speaks in idioms; Holden speaks with sarcasm; Holden speaks for a generation.

Form 7: An intentional sentence fragment or very short sentence

It's hard to demonstrate the power of a deliberate fragment out of context (though I've used this one throughout this book), but here it goes:

- The boys on the island are almost all capable of some sort of self-reflection. Piggy, Ralph, Simon—all are able to consider their own strengths and weaknesses.
  But not Jack.

- What sets Elizabeth Bennet apart from her peers? Wit and intelligence, nothing more.

More Forms: Variations on Forms 1–7

One might vary many of these constructions simply by rearranging the placement of modifiers, series, or repetitions. An introductory appositive, for instance, might be used with a colon or dash at the start of a sentence (*Appositives—they can also start sentences*) or a series might be placed in the middle of a sentence (*Macbeth's greatest weaknesses—ambition, obsession, compulsion—are early on his strengths*). One might also combine one of these sentences with rhetorical devices such as metaphor or allusion to great effect. Encourage students to collect sentences they find intriguing and add them to this barrel; this is also a good opportunity to review some grammatical terms, but mainly, it's an opportunity to create a love of the sentence itself, of what it can achieve and offer to a writer.

Revision Using Advanced Sentence Forms

Here are some suggestions for helping students fill a barrel with sentence models and use those models judiciously.

- Obviously, a first step upon presenting a form is to have students try it themselves, not just in the abstract, but with an actual sentence or idea from a first draft. Practicing in this way gives an opportunity to talk about placement and context; it's not enough to write a complicated sentence, students must also know when and why they're using such a sentence.

- Along the lines of *why*, it's a good idea to reinforce the idea that syntax is not an end in itself, but a means to an end. Let's revisit the first rule I suggested in discussing syntax: **sophisticated sentences lead to sophisticated thinking**. A main benefit of advanced forms, I've found, is that they force students to move toward such sophisticated thinking. Take, for instance, a series of balanced pairs. A student's original sentence might look like this:

My trip to Africa introduced me to extreme poverty and disease.

> If you ask the student to expand this thought using a series of balanced pairs, he or she *must* come up with more to say. Here's one more pair with nice repetition:

My trip to Africa introduced me to extreme poverty and disease, to dying children and dying cities.

> And finally, remember that the pairs work nicely when one adds drama to the last pair by making it abstract, of greater importance, or contrasting:

My trip to Africa introduced me to extreme poverty and disease, to dying children and dying cities, to despair for individuals and hope for nations.

> It works with many of the forms—for that reason, I often suggest that students consider one of the forms, or a combination of them, when constructing a thesis. The form itself may help to create the sophisticated ideas that can improve the argument of an entire paper.

- As part of a discussion about syntax, you might wish to throw in some practice distinguishing *loose* sentences from *periodic* sentences. The difference, simply put: in a loose sentence you can put the period somewhere before the end of the sentence, in a periodic sentence, you can't. Periodic sentences can be tools for building suspense. Remember that famous first sentence of *Pride and Prejudice*? Periodic. The first sentence of *A Tale of Two Cities*? Definitely loose. Here's an example using one of the samples from Form 2 of our barrel. The original read:

The most famous lovers of English literature—Romeo and Juliet, Lancelot and Guinevere, Antony and Cleopatra—all had to overcome obstacles to their love in order to be together.

- Made periodic:

The most famous lovers of English literature (Romeo and Juliet, Lancelot and Guinevere, Antony and Cleopatra), in order to be together, had to overcome great obstacles.

- Assign students to find examples of either the forms themselves or just advanced forms they like from professional writing samples—novels, poems, articles, or other sources. Dissect and categorize the sentence types in class. A book of quotations might be a good source, as well—quite often, how lines are constructed makes them as memorable as does what they say.

- Discuss with students genres in which advanced forms might *not* be useful. Take a look at a front-page article from a local newspaper or an article from a popular magazine, for instance. Not only will you probably not see advanced sentence forms, you may not see long sentences or paragraphs. You may, however, see sentence variety and subordination. Discuss the role of syntax in communicating with different audiences and in communicating different kinds of information.

BETWEEN THE LINES: *Grammar, Punctuation, and Revision*

Grammar is to a writer what anatomy is to a sculptor, or the scales to a musician. You may loathe it, it may bore you, but nothing will replace it, and once mastered it will support you like a rock.
—B. J. Chute

No one yet, so far as I know, has invented the perfect system for teaching grammar. Far from it. Many English teachers I know would as soon teach grammar as reptile handling, for good reason—students don't take to comma rules, by and large, any more than English teachers take to letting snakes loose in their classrooms. At the same time, teachers are desperate for students to *know* grammar, to write without the annoying distractions that poor grammar scatters across the page. Reading some student essays is like driving at rush hour in Istanbul: there are rules, but no one's bothering with them. But before you stick piles of essays in a drawer and just hope everyone forgets they ever existed (trust me; it doesn't work), give revision a chance.

The suggestions below are not meant to help you teach grammar, but to have students *revise* for it. They're suggestions, in other words, for the bottom of the revision cone—the proofreading stage.

- Set aside one stage of revision only for grammar and punctuation:
  - Revise for these aspects of writing only after revising for overall ideas and style.
  - At this stage, read papers (you might read them yourself or have students edit one another's papers in peer groups) *only* for grammar and punctuation—no matter how tempting it is, make no other comments.

- Consider how much you're willing to "fix" for a student *before* reading and marking the paper. Once you've started, you can't back down. Sometimes I just mark errors with a highlighter but don't identify them, sometimes I just list the errors I've seen in a paper but don't mark them individually, sometimes I help students proofread carefully—it depends on the assignment, the stage of revision, the potential audience, and, frankly, on the student. Some students earn my help in this way and seem willing to learn from it, others don't, and while I try not to discriminate, I'll proofread for a student who's written five drafts before I'll proofread for a student who's written only one.

- You might even slow down more and focus on one or two elements of grammar or punctuation at a time. I've found that it sometimes helps to review commas, have students rewrite papers making changes only to comma usage, and then grade those revisions and discuss the changes.

- Make sure students understand the reasons behind grammar rules as well as the rules themselves. Okay, I realize how complicated that statement is—*how* to get students to understand grammar rules is a topic for other books entirely. Nonetheless, the point is sound; true revision will only come when students understand how grammar works as a series of signals to a reader and apply those signals thoughtfully.

- For the purpose of revision, have students pay particular attention to marks of punctuation that help a sentence deliver its meaning with drama or connection: semicolons, colons, and dashes. Try, for instance, having students simply mark with colors every instance in an essay where one of these marks occurs, and five where one *could* occur. Then students can decide whether or not to make such changes and what those changes would accomplish.

- Reading aloud is always a good idea. Okay, so you feel like an idiot reading your own work to a wall—for some of us, it's the best audience we can hope for. The wall doesn't criticize, smirk, or tell you your sentences are weak, but your own voice just might. Suggest to students that they read papers out loud to themselves or to others to catch mistakes at the proofreading stage.

- I tried this one once with a friend's economics paper simply because I didn't understand any more of what he was saying one way or another: read the entire paper backwards. Strangely,

continued

it works for some errors. You lose any sense of content but see words in groups and phrases—you also see punctuation more obviously. The friend, by the way, got a D on the paper, but I don't think it was because of proofreading; the professor didn't seem to think my friend made any more sense economically than I did. On the other hand, by now my friend is probably rich as Midas, and I'm still locating comma splices and split infinitives in other people's writing. Go figure.

- Try this method of peer editing at the proofreading stage: put students in groups, but change the groupings often. You might, for instance, have groups of students help edit and proofread one another's introductions. Then switch all of the groups around and work on second paragraphs; repeat the process until papers have been checked all the way through. This way, if one group doesn't catch the errors in a student's paper, another group might catch a recurrence of the error, thus helping the student recognize the first mistake, as well. Similarly, you might have a first grouping read only for comma errors, a second only for apostrophes, and so forth—if nothing else, this keeps things interesting for the students.

Actually, students who have worked hard to revise the ideas, style, and overall scope of papers may just be more likely to *want* to revise grammar and punctuation. They may also wish to revise if they know there will be an audience other than an English teacher armed with a red pen and a vicious streak reading the final product. Proofreading is never fun, but sometimes it seems more necessary than others, and sometimes you just feel that you have to do it. Who knows? Maybe at some point the papers will arrive with better grammar and punctuation in the first place, and you won't find yourself quite as excited every time you receive junk mail from SPCA because you think this time it just might stand for the Society for the Prevention of Cruelty to Apostrophes, not animals, and more than a little disappointed when you realize you're wrong.

WITH A TWIST: *Turns of Phrase*

If, with the literate, I am
Impelled to try an epigram,
I never seek to take the credit;
We all assume that Oscar said it.
                    —Dorothy Parker

If there's anyone who could turn a phrase half as well as Oscar Wilde, it was Dorothy Parker. One could list the wonders of their comments and ripostes all day. Even on his deathbed, Wilde reportedly managed a quip: "This wallpaper is killing me; one of us has got to go." Parker, in a review, once wrote, "This is not a novel to be tossed aside lightly. It should be thrown with great force."

Not all turns of phrase need to be humorous, though they generally require at least a bit of cleverness. Turns of phrase play on the expectations of the reader, on the idioms of our language and our familiarity with it. They enliven writing, sometimes by complicating a plain phrase to make it witty, and sometimes just by making a complicated meaning more plain. See?

And if you're thinking students can't learn to turn a phrase, that some of us are just witty or clever and others of us aren't, think again.

Here, as proof, are lines written in class by students:

- I thought *Beowulf* was a pretty good book, at first, but after a while I realized that he was just pretty and good, and it was just a book.

- Elizabeth Bennet walked a few miles through the rain to get to Bingley's house, and I, like everyone around her, wished she'd kept walking.

- The other day I compared a friend of mine to a dog, but I should really apologize—to my dog.

And, not quite as meanly:

- In the end, Beowulf was killed by the most vicious monster of all—old age.

- Jack pretends to really dislike Algernon as a friend, and dislikes him for real when they pretend to be brothers.

- Finally, please let me in to your college because my parents made me a promise—I can't give you one of those sob stories about how I'd be the first in my family to go to college, but I'd be the first to go in my own car.

Sometimes the most fun I have working on revision with classes is practicing and thinking about turns of phrase. I don't know if Oscar Wilde and Dorothy Parker came up with every retort and joke on the spot (Wilde, in particular, seemed to turn phrases as easily as turning corners), but I suspect even they occasionally saved a good one for just the right occasion. The rest of us often have to work at it. With that in mind, I devote class time, after students have written a first draft (or two), to working on and sharing some clever turns of phrase.

Having Your Way with Words: Rules for Revision

To begin with, I point out to students that verbal humor can, by and large, be categorized. There are, of course, many kinds of humor in the literature we read, ranging from puns to dramatic irony and slapstick, but it's fairly easy to narrow down a few reproducible effects one can achieve with a single phrase. A few categories:

- *A play on words.* Students get puns ("Dickens spit a lot—he had *great expectorations . . .*"), but not all plays on words need be silly witticisms. Novelist Jeannette Winterson, for instance, said of the term *post-impressionism* that the "twentieth century would soon be entirely fenced in with posts." I once received an essay in which a student wrote of *The Grapes of Wrath*, "The Joads travel hundreds of miles to collect, not just figuratively but literally, the fruits of their labors."

- *Chiasmus.* Sometimes, flipping the elements of a sentence flips the meaning of those elements, as well—nouns become verbs, verbs nouns, even if slight modifications need to be made. Another example from a student: "If you spend your life making money, there's no time to spend your money on life."

- *The unexpected specification.* Quite often a simple aphorism, or even just an average statement, can come to life if you add a qualification or specification at the end—the one thing that statement doesn't apply to, or perhaps the one thing it does: "All experience is good for writers—except for physical pain" (William Trevor). Another favorite: "The remarkable thing about Shakespeare is that he is really very good—in spite of all the people who say he is very good" (Robert Graves).

- *Analogy and metaphor.* Analogies, along with similes and metaphors, work best if the comparison is surprising but apt; "Poetry," said John Wain, "is to prose as dancing is to walking." Many good turns of phrase come from a comparison in which the point is obvious only once the writer has explained it: "Writing is like getting married. One should never commit oneself until one is amazed at one's luck" (Iris Murdoch). I like also Robert Frost's explanation of why he stuck to form: "I'd as soon write free verse as play tennis with the net down."

- *Changes to a single word (or two).* When Marianne Moore was told by a reader that her poetry was "difficult to read," she responded, "It is very difficult to write." Quite often a plain sentence, repeated with only a word or two changed, becomes a clever insight. Again, a second example: "Novels are about other people and poems are about yourself" (Philip Larkin).

- *Unexpected definitions.* Writers love to define their own art. H. L. Mencken, for one, defined poetry as "a comforting piece of fiction set to more or less lascivious music"; Matthew Arnold called it "a criticism of

life"; Percy Bysshe Shelley called poets themselves "the unacknowl-
edged legislators of the world." Students, too, are capable of the surprising definition, as this example shows: "What is a novel, after all, other
than a desperate attempt to control time?"

One might easily come up with more; I've had students peruse anthologies and
books of quotations and come up with a short list of favorites which we then
work together to categorize further. In this case, modeling is crucial; even
comedians work on their routines, and most of us aren't always as clever
immediately as we can be with a bit of preparation. For that reason, revision,
too, is crucial. In fact, of all of the aspects of writing covered in this book, crafting turns of phrase may be the single skill most suited to revision and not first
drafts, since it requires, for many, a good deal of thought.

That's not to say that, with practice, students don't get better at twisting
words a bit—they do. Students might also remember their better efforts and
reuse them without shame, filling up a barrel of turns of phrase for use on
future essays that focus on a similar subject or work.

Here are a few easy and fun steps for encouraging students to try their
hands at turning a phrase:

1. Ask students to look through a first draft and underline or circle any
    simple statements, aphorisms, and short sentences that might need spic-
    ing up. Ask them, too, to look closely at their introduction, conclusion,
    and the last sentence of each paragraph—if any sentence seems in need
    of a bit more punch, ask them to underline it.

2. Next, have students reexamine the underlined sentences and pick out
    the most important words. Let's say, for instance, that a student found
    this sentence in an original draft: "Hamlet pretends to be mad when he
    sees Ophelia at the play." The key words? The verb, of course: *pretends*.
    Mad. *Play*, perhaps.

3. Ask students to consider the underlined words. What other meanings
    do they have? *Play* has an obvious second meaning and other double
    meanings that accompany it, such as *acting* and *stage*. So does *mad*.
    There's not much else to do with *pretends*, though it might occur to the
    writer that actors in a play are pretending, as well.

4. Now offer some choices:

    • Flip the elements in the sentence, paying special attention to the
      underlined words—can they be used, rearranged, or altered a bit to
      imply greater meaning? Perhaps, for instance, one might suggest that
      "Hamlet acts out of madness, but his madness is an act" or that
      "Hamlet plays at madness, and madly concocts a play."

- Make a play on one of the words in some way: "Hamlet's play is just that—not only a production on stage, but a game of pretending to be mad."

- Repeat the phrase, changing a single underlined word: "Hamlet acts mad when he sees Ophelia, he is mad when he sees his mother."

- Make an analogy out of the sentence: "Hamlet pretends to be mad just as the players pretend to be kings and queens."

Practice helps—when one gets in the habit of looking for possible phrases to turn, they become more apparent. Students like the exercise; the next time they read Wilde or Parker, they're more likely to get the jokes, too. And not every revision exercise need be successful every time for students to get the ideas. After all, "experience," as Oscar Wilde defined it, "is the name everyone gives to their mistakes."

CAN YOU HEAR ME NOW?: *Finding Voice*

> *What I am trying to achieve is a voice sitting by a fireplace telling you a story on a winter's evening.*
>
> —Truman Capote

You've hung in this long, so permit me, if you will, one more cooking metaphor. I'm not sure I've ever actually baked a cake, but I know how it's done; I've certainly eaten my fair share, and I know, too, that it's not as easy as simply following a recipe. A cake is more than the sum of its parts: you start with flour, sugar, and baking powder, but what you end up with is not just a collection of those ingredients but something new entirely, *a cake*. There's a delicate process involved, too, as I understand it—you don't just lump it all in a bowl and toss it in the oven, unless you anticipate a product that would taste like *I* made it.

So, you can connect the dots from syntax and diction to grammar, imagery, tone, organization, but you won't get a complete picture from looking at the individual elements. The elusive quality of writing called *voice*—a concept so abstract, really, that many writing teachers throw up their hands in despair at the idea of teaching it—can't be discovered, demonstrated, or defined by any one aspect of writing or revision. But I don't believe that voice is simply a quality a writer naturally has or doesn't have, either. I think revision is a place to hone and refine the writer's voice, and that ignoring voice just because it's a difficult concept is like leaving the batter in the bowl without actually baking the cake.

We know, of course, when we come across a piece of writing that has voice, one that sounds uniquely like the student who wrote the words:

If I try, and try, and think about it, I guess I'd have to say that when I was seven, the risk of getting on a jet-ski was a risk that led to "significant change and discovery" in my life. Actually, it wasn't so much getting on the jet-ski that changed my life; it was the event that happened while I was on the jet-ski.

I don't really remember what happened, so I have to rely on sources comparable to *World Weekly News* and *The National Enquirer*: my parents (I mean really, how can I trust the people who lied to me for over 12 years about a fat, jolly communist?). From their perspective, I got on the back seat of the jet-ski being driven by a ten-year-old girl; she made a sharp turn, I fell off and hit a speed-boat head-on.

—Jared Herring

It's not that the opening of Jared's essay sounds individual because I know Jared; there's something in this piece of writing that gives you a feeling of a real person behind it. Is it the jokes? The syntax? The casual tone? The details? No one element of Jared's introductory paragraphs creates the sense of a narrator who's an actual person; the combination of elements matters. Certainly one can imagine the student essay that answers the same prompt *without* an individual voice:

A time I faced a significant change and discovery in my life was the time I fell off a jet-ski and was hit by a speed-boat. I was seven years old and the driver was a ten-year-old girl. My terrified parents watched the whole thing.

That's all Jared's told us, really, but we have much more sense of Jared as a writer, as a speaker, in his own piece than in my scaled-down rendition.

A big part of writing a personal essay—a personal anything, for that matter, from an email to a Nobel Prize speech—is infusing the writing with voice. Writing a formal essay, an academic piece, raises the stakes even higher. Can you even have a voice in a formal essay? It's so *formal*.

I say yes. I also say you can strengthen voice in revision. You will never create a student's voice for the student; you may even be frustrated that students who have unique and exciting voices when they speak or write, say, fiction, produce some of the stiffest and most common prose you've read in a formal assignment. Finding voice takes practice, true, but it also requires risk and will. It's easier to write stiffly; no one expects much of you. As soon as you start to create a voice, you put yourself into your piece, and everything, including criticism, becomes personal.

Take the book you're holding, for instance. I've discussed the voice with my editor, with readers, with my wife. I've made deliberate choices, like addressing you as a *you* and revealing my deep love for but lack of practical knowledge about cake. I've *revised* for voice, asking myself tough questions: Is this joke stupid? Too stupid to leave in? Is this section boring? Do I sound like a real teacher here? Should I devote an entire paragraph to talking about my own voice, or will that just sound self-aggrandizing and draw attention to the flaws in what I write? And the real kicker is, I'll probably never know the answers. But I can do my best to make the voice convincing, and much of that work is accomplished in revision.

Revising for Voice

Holden Caulfield opens the first sentence of *Catcher in the Rye* with the phrase "if you really want to know about it" and closes it with the phrase "if you want to know the truth." It's that "really" that sticks out when I reread Salinger's novel; Holden frequently insists that what he says is "real" and "true," implying that he's no "phony." There's a double point to bringing this up. First of all, Salinger created one of the greatest voices in the canon of high school literature—maybe all literature—when he created Holden, and I'm certain he didn't do it without revising.

I also think Holden is worried about his own voice in the same way all great storytellers are. He wants to be honest, to sound honest and authentic, but at the same time he knows (at least subconsciously, I'd argue) that the role of a narrator involves a certain amount of manipulation of facts, details, and language. The choices one makes in such manipulation are at least a part of how voice is created.

Moving a piece of writing, especially a formal, academic piece, toward an authentic and honest voice is no small challenge. The tips that follow may serve as a start in helping students revise for voice:

- Ask students to look back over a draft that's as close to "final" as it can be and ask these questions:
  - Is the voice consistent? Does it sound like it was written by the same person and with the same attention to each part?
  - Do you have the sense of a real person speaking from reading the piece? If not, why not?
  - Do you sense that the speaker cares about what he or she is saying?
  - Do you *want* to keep reading the piece as it progresses?
  - Does the writing promote some reaction—good or bad—from the reader?
  - Is the voice appropriate to the audience?
  - Is the language fresh and original or trite and common?
- If a formal paper feels stiff and wooden, give students these instructions: Try going back and thinking through the paper as if it used "I" regularly. Imagine how a personal essay on the same topic might alter the wording and phrases. You might even rewrite the essay using the first person, then go back and take "I" or other first person pronouns out.

- Try having students write about the same topic in a completely different format—fast-writing, writing an email or letter, or preparing for an oral report. Than have them try to combine that voice with the organization of a formal paper.

- Have students try to put themselves in the position of an audience. You might even have them write reactions, reflections, or criticisms about their own work as if they were reading it for the first time.

- Line up a paragraph from a student paper beside a paragraph from a professional writing sample. Ask the author to examine both and reflect on the differences before rewriting. If the paper is an essay, try lining up the student sample by, say, an article of criticism or encyclopedia topic on the same subject. It's possible, by the way, that the student sample should contain a more individualized voice than the professional sample—a dictionary or encyclopedia is not generally known for its engaging and personal style.

- Ask students to create a persona for the speaker other than the real author—even for a formal paper. Make a list as a class of possible identities, noting that these identities need not be mentioned or even readily evidenced in the paper, but may inform other choices made by the author. The persona need not be wildly different from the actual writer's identity—simply suggesting that one imagine writing as a young professor trying to engage a class of reluctant physics students in a discussion of *King Lear* or as a professional plumber assigned his first essay in a graduate course on *Moby Dick* might suggest new modes of expression, metaphor, or analysis to students and help them to create voice.

- Go back and reexamine specific elements of the paper such as syntax, diction, punctuation, evidence, and organization with the idea of voice in mind. If the paper is stiff and boring, ask if there are other choices that could be made that are still appropriate for the format. Could the paper start in a different way? Could the syntax vary the rhythm or tone of the voice more?

Revision for the Teacher: Voice and the Assignments We Make

There's a modern movement, I believe, away from requiring that essays never be written in first person, that the pronoun "I" be banned from formal writing. I have mixed feelings about the rule. On the one hand, there's good reason to exclude the first person from formal essays written by students: students can weaken their argument with sentences that start out "I believe," as if belief replaces the need for evidence. At the same time, it's rare to read professional writing that doesn't recognize the "I" behind the piece. Even formal criticism can use a distanced first person approach if handled well.

When we consider the audience in making writing assignments, one question we're helping to clear up for the writer is the question of appropriate voice. And not every assignment need fall squarely into the realm of pure formal criticism or personal essay. Consider offering students a specific task in their writing—"You are writing an in-depth criticism of this work for the *New York Times* (and here's a sample to go by)," or "You must compose a speech on *Othello* to be delivered to one hundred Shakespearean scholars who know the play intimately." Such assignments, based on possible real-world tasks, take into account the possibility that personal experience and objective scholarship might mingle in one composition, and in so doing promote the use of voice in academic writing.

At the same time, when making an assignment you might consider whether or not some approaches are appropriate and discuss those possibilities with students beforehand. How about dialogue, jokes, and personal experience? Also consider other ways of letting the information in; I recently allowed a student to add a preface to a research-based formal essay on characters who martyr themselves for a cause, and the result was that the rather straightforward analysis took on fantastic overtones:

> Two years ago, I decided it was time to watch the crucifixions in Santa Maria just past the Olongapo borders, and far beyond the naval base on which I lived in the Philippines. When we first stepped foot outside our car, we heard a quiet chanting of the Lord's Prayer, and cries of pain, and I thought I'd missed the event altogether. I rushed up the dirt street to the side of a small shack, and pushed my way through the crowd so that I could see what was happening. A line of men in only red rag shorts were walking slowly, to the rhythm of the peoples' chanting of the "Our Father," and each was carrying a thick rod with seven long strings hanging off of it, each with a sharp piece of metal at the end, and every man threw it over his shoulder in a whipping motion every four steps, switching sides every time.
>
> —*Alexandra Fisher*

I'd hate to have missed allowing Alex the chance to share this experience and reason for writing the paper. At the same time, the experience didn't need to crop up, suddenly, in the middle of her discussion on John Proctor. The compromise not only made the paper more interesting without damaging its integrity, it also taught Alex a lesson about organizing material on a larger scale than a single essay as we discussed the role of a preface, an appendix, and footnotes.

In the end, teaching students that their voices can leap from the page as well as they carry in a school hallway is partly the responsibility of the assignment and the way it's presented. Revision can help; a student who struggles just to get words onto the page might need to write with an "I" for more distance before editing; in personal essays, just the opposite might be true. In time, one hopes, all student writers will discover that Holden didn't need to be concerned, that we as an audience *do* want to know the truth, that we do really want to hear what our students really have to say.

4 *Getting It Together*

Peer and Class Revision Strategies

No passion in the world is equal to the passion to alter someone else's draft.

—H. G. Wells

If misery loves company, I've often thought, then it's strange that so many writers work alone. I've known authors who love what they do but loathe what they write while they're doing it; writers can be their own worst critics. But the expression for writers might be rephrased; perhaps it's revision that loves company. Many of the strategies in this book can be used by authors to revise their own work, but in many cases it takes a fresh set of eyes—and ears—to point out flaws or strengths. Revision suggestions by others can offer validation, call us on the choices we hoped to get away with, alert us to errors or omissions we missed, and give us the chance to review our words in ways we might not have thought about otherwise.

This chapter offers a catalog of assignments and methods for structuring the revision process in your classes. The ideas that follow are not meant to form a checklist or overall system; you can pick and choose from these techniques as you like. Roughly, however, the ideas below fall into three categories of activity:

- *Peer revision activities*: Reading Aloud, Peer Revision in Pairs, Peer Revision in Groups, Writing and Revision in Groups

- *Individual revision activities to use with an entire class*: Reading Aloud, Color Marking, Metacognition, Limited Focus Revision, De-outlining, Looping, Cutting and Pasting, Shortening the Word Count, Litmus Tests, Typing

- *Assessment ideas and approaches*: Teacher-Student Conferencing, Student-Generated Rubrics and Revision Systems, Zero Tolerance Grading, Publication

For ideas of how to combine, stagger, or alternate between these activities throughout a course, see Appendix A at the end of this book, "A Sample Plan for Teaching Revision in a Semester."

Peer Revision Activities

Reading Aloud

Reading a paper aloud offers the chance to catch mechanical errors and issues of voice and content. I often suggest to students that they read written work to friends, parents, or even just to themselves—or, better yet, that they have a friend or parent read to them. A few guidelines I suggest:

- If the reader stumbles or pauses at all, stop and mark the paper at that spot.

- If the reader or listener notices a repeating issue (repeated use of the same word, for instance), mark the issue once, then ignore it for the rest of the reading—the author can clean the rest up later.

- Once a listener has heard the paper read aloud, ask this question: "What is the point of this piece?"

- Then ask: "What works in this piece?" The answers to this question and the one above will often reveal much about what *doesn't* work, as well.

- Ignore spelling errors. These can be cleaned up by hand.

Working in Pairs

I've heard many student complaints about peer revision activities. Too often, a student's experience with peer revision has resulted in little or no improvement to a final draft. That doesn't mean peer revision doesn't work, however. In fact, if nothing else, peer revision is effective simply because students need to read and hear each other's voices in order to improve their own writing. With some planning, however, peer revision can be immediately effective as well:

- Be deliberate but careful in the way you match up students. Try not to create a hierarchy of "good" and "bad" writers—mix pairings up in various ways.

- Create time in class for students to read papers aloud to each other. Authors will benefit both from reading their work aloud and from listening to their work read aloud by a partner.

- Give specific instructions for paired reading. Specify, for example:
  - The stage of revision—whether students should read for overall argument and organization or simply for mechanical errors;
  - A few specific aspects, such as syntax or verb use, to look for;
  - Whether or not students are allowed to interrupt the reading to point out flaws, ask questions, or compliment well-written passages;
  - Whether or not spelling mistakes should be pointed out at this stage.

- Focus on parts rather than the whole. Try having pairs work only on an introduction, then discuss the process of writing an introduction as a class before moving on to the body of a paper.

Workshop Groups

Most of the methods used for partnered revision can be expanded for group activities, but groups entail a different dynamic than pairs. Submitting writing to the scrutiny of a group can be intimidating for even the best writers—commenting on someone else's work before a group can be intimidating, too. Groups more easily get off task and more easily gang up on an author. But a good workshopping group provides numerous benefits—a support network, the opportunity to see multiple examples of response to an assignment, and many sets of eyes on a single paper. At their best, groups offer students the chance to discuss technical aspects of writing in a way they might never do as a full class.

A few tips to remember about having students work in groups:

- Groups work best if they are given specific guidelines and instructions.

- Space matters, and so does size—orchestrate groups so that they can comfortably sit in a circle, all facing one another and all physically equal. I like groups of three to five students each.

- Groups will get off-task. Sometimes this is okay—you want group members to be comfortable, to enjoy the process, and to establish a level of trust. You don't want them to stray so far that they aren't productive. Try to find a balance.

- It's intimidating for groups to hear what other groups are saying. In a small class, I sometimes put on background music, send groups into the hallway to work, or look for other ways to make the group discussion more private.

- Groups work better when each member of the group has his or her own copy of the work under discussion.

I do have a few firm rules for group review and revision. Here's the general procedure I ask groups to use with each new paper:

- Someone—the author, or another group member if the author prefers—reads the entire paper aloud.

- The author does not speak until the group has finished its initial comments.

- First comments should always point out strengths of the paper and should be phrased positively.

- After some of the paper's strengths have been pointed out, the groups should discuss general organization and argumentation.

- Minor technical issues such as spelling and punctuation can simply be marked on the paper—these need be discussed only if they are consistent or problematic.

- After the group has discussed the paper, the author has a chance to ask questions or explain (explanations, however, almost always indicate a need for revision—if the group didn't "get it" from the reading, there's probably a problem in the writing).

- At the end of the discussion, each group member should hand his or her copy of the work to the author with any marks or general comments included. Often, comments will be included that did not even come up in the discussion.

Revising in Groups

Writing is a solitary art. It's tough for many writers to put words together with others, but revision with others can be a worthwhile process. Group revision often results in discussion of alternatives and approaches.

Try asking students to work in groups to rewrite sentences or paragraphs that you devise or take (anonymously, perhaps) from student essays.

Individual Revision Activities

Color Marking

Color marking is just what it sounds like—students mark elements of their drafts in different colors. Even without colors, students can identify two elements consistently by circling or underlining, but there's something about marking up a whole draft in a rainbow of colors that makes revision more fun.

To begin with, ask students to highlight or underline a combination of these aspects of the draft with a different color:

- verbs
- adjectives
- the first four words of every sentence (syntax)
- marks of punctuation other than periods and commas
- rhetorical devices or other interesting turns of phrase
- supporting evidence

Once you've singled out an element, discuss approaches with the class and revise one piece at a time—improve the verbs only or rewrite for syntax (see the discussion about limiting the focus of revision in the next section).

A few other ideas you might consider:

- Try both positive color marking (marking what the reader thinks is good about the piece) and negative color marking (marking what the reader thinks needs correction or improvement)—but be clear about which approach you're using.

- Have partners color mark one another's papers.

- Try a color-marking system where everything in the paper gets a color— mark short, medium, and long sentences in different colors, for instance, or sentences that contain evidence and those that analyze in two shades.

- Assign colors to each item on a student-generated rubric. Instead of making comments, just color mark papers and hand them back for revision—students will have to refer to the rubric (by color) to make corrections and improvements.

Limited Focus Revision

Most teachers recognize the fact that students have trouble rewriting a paper that sports a sea of circled errors, marginal corrections, and general notes. The tendency when faced with an overwhelming number of comments on a paper is to fix the simplest, most obvious mistakes and ignore the rest; important overall suggestions may go unheeded.

One answer is to force yourself (it's tough, I know) to have students focus on only one or two areas of revision at a time. There are various ways to think about limiting focus:

- Mark first drafts only for content and with substantive suggestions. Then mark second drafts for one or two specific areas—punctuation and syntax only, for instance. Continue with drafts until all necessary areas of the paper have been revised.

- Consider using limited focus revision as a stepping-stone process throughout the year—revise all first papers for some mistakes, then on the next paper expect those areas to be correct, but ask for revision on a new small set of errors, and so on.

- Use color marking to identify all of the types of errors or likely areas for revision in a paper at once, but then revise just one area at a time.

Metacognition

Metacognition—the process of thinking about one's own thinking—is invaluable to the writer, and many of the exercises in this book lead students in this direction. At least once a semester, however, I like to make an assignment that asks students to engage in metacognition without a specific assignment in mind; in other words, I ask them to think about the overall process of their learning and development as writers. The assignment might be simply to answers a few questions like these:

- How has your writing improved this semester?
- What areas of weakness remain—where does your writing still need work?
- What do you enjoy about writing?
- What is most challenging to you as a writer (not necessarily a weakness in your writing—this could have to do with process or engagement)?
- What has changed since you last completed this sort of reflection for this class?

You can also try using metacognition with individual revision assignments. Ask students to describe in a separate assignment how they revised a piece and why, using specific examples. The process of discussing process often makes for interesting class discussions and better writing the next time around.

De-outlining

The place of outlining as a prewriting activity has been firmly established for so long that I imagine ancient Egyptian instructors glaring over the shoulders of their students at walls of hieroglyphics and muttering, "I *told* you to work harder on the outline." Other methods of prewriting, such as webbing, clustering, and cubing, are now used to encourage students in the same way—to plan, to organize, and to brainstorm before starting to write.

For revision purposes, the same tools can be effective used in reverse—students can de-outline or de-web a paper to check for structure. Having a class make an outline of papers that have already been composed in draft form can be revealing—it's sometimes easy to see what's missing or imbalanced. Gaps in logic or lack of evidence often become visually apparent.

You might also try having revision partners try to de-outline one another's papers, then discuss. Problems with transitions, the logical flow of arguments, or paragraph lengths often come to light through this approach.

Looping

I've heard the process of looping attributed to any number of works, but I first encountered the method in the classroom of my own high school English teacher, Bill Brown, decades ago. Bill used looping primarily in creative writing assignments, for poetry or stories or personal essays.

The looping technique works like this: Students fast-write a first draft. Then each author reads through his or her fast-write, circling any areas that seem promising, suggest other stories or important points, or stand out in some other way. Each student then chooses one of the circled areas or phrases and starts a new draft from that point. The process can continue again and again, for as long as necessary.

What's accomplished by looping? Focus, clarity, weeding out extraneous argumentation or background. Take a personal essay: a student might start out by writing about how great, generally, a year-long basketball season was, but wind up with a tightly focused description of a single play in a single game.

Cutting and Pasting

Have students cut out each paragraph, section, or sentence of a composition and paste it on a separate sheet of paper (I like to do this with scissors and tape, though it can be done electronically with a word processing program). Then consider:

- Could the composition afford to lose the first paragraph entirely? Many personal essays and stories can.

- What happens if the paragraphs (or sentences) are shuffled into a different order? Does the paper flow logically and organically from beginning to end?

- Is the conclusion strong?

- Are the units roughly balanced in terms of length, evidence, and importance? If not, is that deliberate?

Shortening the Word Count

Seniors working on college essays often discover that a second application requires a word count half as long as a first application; suddenly, they need to chop an essay drastically. It's a good exercise, one that often results in a strong second draft of the essay. There are two steps for such reduction—first look for individual words and phrases to cut or condense and then search out entire sentences or paragraphs that can go.

Consider lowering the word count for a second draft in one of these ways:

- Simply lower the entire word count for the paper—from five hundred to four hundred words, for instance;

- Require that students cut a certain number of words from each paragraph (you might stipulate, at the same time, a *minimum* number of words in each sentence).

Litmus Tests

Earlier in this book, I discussed using models before students write. Think about modeling as a step toward revision, as well. After one or more drafts are complete, go back and look at good examples of the style and genre of writing. How does the draft compare? What's lacking in the draft that the model accomplishes? Is there anything the draft does better than the model?

Litmus tests work well in reviewing voice. Compare an essay to an encyclopedia entry, to a critical essay by a recognized scholar, and to a feature from a journal or magazine. Which voice most closely approximates the voice in the student's writing? Which would the student most wish to sound like? What revision strategy can help accomplish that goal?

Typing

Most of the students I teach type their work. I've devoted an entire chapter of this book to ways you can use technology in the process of revision. However, consider this one too: type the piece over. Whether a student is working from a handwritten draft or a typed draft, typing a piece (again) forces the author to slow down, reconsider words and sentences, and revisit ideas.

Assessment Ideas and Approaches

Teacher-Student Conferencing

I usually have good intentions about conferencing with all of my students individually while the class is engaged in other activities such as group work or solitary writing. The truth is that I wind up holding student "conferences" during my planning period, after school, before school, at lunch, by email, outside the teacher's lounge—wherever a student can find me. But there's a difference between glancing at a paper to answer a specific question and holding a more formal conference—it's worth keeping in mind that every student deserves individual attention paid to his or her writing at least once in a while.

I like to set some guidelines for conferences so that the students and I both have a similar level of expectation and a shared comfort zone. Here are some of the guidelines I use for myself:

- The point of a conference is not for me to fix or revise a paper. I make suggestions and discuss the direction of a piece of writing, but I don't mark specific errors except as examples for further revision.

- I always begin with questions:
  - What kind of prewriting did you do and how did it help?
  - What is your overall goal or argument in this piece?
  - Where do you think the paper needs help or work?
  - Are you happy with the introduction and conclusion?
  - What revision strategies are you planning on using?
  - How much time have you set aside for revision?

- I try to frame every comment as a suggestion, not a command—students deserve to retain the choices of authorship.

- I never compare one student's writing to another's, but I do try to compare student writing to that of professional authors, to anonymous models we've discussed in class, and to other works by the same student.

- I try to ask about process as well as content in a conference. I need students to think about time, strategy, and the learning process.

- I always end the conference by summing up—or better yet, asking the student to summarize—what's been said and the specific steps that the student should follow from that point on.

As for the guidelines I use with students, they vary. I always remind them of the first point in my list, that the point of a conference is not to fix simple errors. At times (especially for second conferences on the same paper), I insist that the student prepare questions or points of discussion. I also insist, regularly, that students come to a first conference with some material in hand—even if a student hasn't prepared a first draft, he or she should have a thesis written down and some ideas about how to proceed. I don't allow students to say, for instance, "I want to write about fate. What should I do?" *Fate* is not a thesis—it's not even a theme. My mother, the English teacher, once said to me, "It's like a student saying, 'I want to write about *arm*.' Everybody's got one. Big deal."

Student-Generated Rubrics and Revision Systems

If the goal of revision activities is to create vested interest in improving writing among authors, then students deserve to have a say in the structures by which their work and processes are judged. In the case of both grading rubrics and systems for revising drafts, there's no reason students *shouldn't* be involved in creating these structures.

Start with some simple questions and then have a class or groups of students come up with answers:

- What elements should be the focus of our revision and in what order?

- What elements should be the focus of grading?

- How much of the grade should each of the elements be worth? Should they all be weighted equally?

- What is the teacher's responsibility (what should I mark or comment on and what should I ignore in this draft)?

- What is the student's responsibility (what are you accountable for and when does the failure to live up to your responsibility mean that I should stop grading and simply fail the paper or stop reading it)?

- What should the full process of revision look like—how many drafts will be required or allowed? What's the timetable?

The most important thing about a student-generated rubric or revision system is that you stick to it. You can always set some nonnegotiable rules—I deserve a say in my own role and in that of the students—and you can help with the structure and organization of the rubric, especially with younger students. The following are some examples of student-generated rubrics from my own classes.

Student-Generated Rubric 1

Essays will be assessed in four areas; each area is worth 25 percent of your grade.

1. Content: Did you choose a good, interesting, and original thesis? Did you support this thesis with good evidence, come to a reasonable and insightful conclusion, and relate your ideas to overall meaning?	Between 0 and 25
2. Quality of writing: Is the writing clear, stylistically interesting, without awkwardness and errors of syntax?	Between 0 and 25 (−5 points per error or teacher comment)
3. Organization: Is the paper well-organized, with clear transitions, a logical flow, and a good introduction and conclusion?	Between 0 and 25
4. Mechanics: Is the paper technically and grammatically correct?	Between 0 and 25 (−3 points per error)

Student-Generated Rubric 2

Each essay will be scored by three other students (papers and graders will remain anonymous) using the following scoring chart. Each time the "below average" column is checked by any reader, the grade will be lowered by three points. Each time the "above average" column is checked, the grade will be raised by three points.

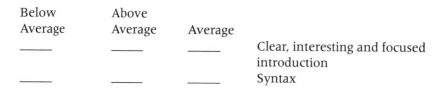

Below Average	Above Average	Average	
_____	_____	_____	Clear, interesting and focused introduction
_____	_____	_____	Syntax

_____	_____	_____	Diction
_____	_____	_____	Use of evidence from the text
_____	_____	_____	Mechanics (grammar, spelling)
_____	_____	_____	Logic of argument
_____	_____	_____	Clear transitions
_____	_____	_____	Clear, interesting, and focused introduction
_____	_____	_____	Overall quality of writing (voice)

Student-Generated Rubric 3

The following rubric was developed through group work in an AP English literature class (in imitation of other AP rubrics and using the nine-point AP grading scale) for essays that analyzed Shakespeare's Sonnet 60.

High-scoring essays

8–9 (A)   These well-written essays clearly answer the question by offering an analysis of the poem that focuses on overall meaning. In addition, they use ample and appropriate supporting evidence from the text and underscore this evidence with sophisticated analysis. While they may have slight errors, they are characterized by clarity, skill in writing, and perceptive ideas. They may take risks in answering the question that pay off in their conclusion.

High-scoring essays correctly identify the various images the speaker uses in the sonnet to lead toward a statement about the inevitability of death and the desire to counteract it through poetry. They note the emphasis of each quatrain on an image related to time's passage: the repetitive and forward-moving nature of the ocean, the growth of humans over time, and the personification of time. High-scoring essays also note the shift in the couplet—from a focus on time's passage to an idea about how the speaker may "conquer" time—and likely note the importance of the phrase "in hope" in casting a shadow of uncertainty on the speaker's claims.

The very best essays may support an analytical thesis not just with interpretations of imagery such as those already noted, but also by correctly identifying more complicated and nuanced aspects of the poem: the cyclical nature of time as suggested by images of the ocean, of "eclipses," and of time's scythe moving its arc; the connection of such cycles to the passage of "our minutes" (the hands of a clock moving in circles); the various puns in the poem, such as the play on "our" and "hour" (underscored by the number of the poem—60), "parallels" (identifying not only wrinkles but also military trenches or even lines of geographic demarcation), "main" (meaning both a key idea and the ocean), and "transfixes" (meaning both to spear and to regard with awe); or the *specific* meanings added to the poem by rhetorical devices such as alliteration (line 10), personification (line 9), or simile (line 1).

7 (B+)   These essays meet all of the requirements of other high-scoring essays, but may be somewhat less developed or perceptive than a higher scoring paper. They may be characterized by correct usage and adequate sentence composition without demonstrating stylistic achievement. Their approach to the relationship between the imagery and the main idea of the poem is likely to be simple and straightforward. They either do not take risks in answering the question or the risks they take do not pay off in the conclusion.

Medium-scoring essays

6 (B–)   These essays answer the question completely without demonstrating particular skill or clarity in writing or perception. They will likely include simple construction, organization, and syntactical strategies. While they do address the imagery of the poem and the idea presented in the couplet, they make the connection in broad strokes with only basic evidence and analysis. They may be minimally developed and lack a probing or thoughtful conclusion.

5 (C+)   These mid-level essays respond to the question without any important errors, but they miss the complexity of the speaker's argument, focusing on only the most obvious aspects of the poem. They may rely on inadequate evidence or have trouble assimilating evidence and analysis into the argument in a smooth fashion. Typically these essays will demonstrate simplistic thinking and only adequate writing skill. Although the writing conveys the writer's thoughts, it will not be as well conceived or developed as upper-half papers.

4 (C–)   These essays will contain most of the elements of a 5 paper, but will likely have important errors or rely on inadequate evidence. They may contain summary in place of analysis. The writing style will demonstrate a lack of clear control over elements such as diction, grammar, and organization. The argument may be flawed by serious misinterpretation or omission, and the papers may not address all aspects of the question directly. They may be quite short and undeveloped.

Low-scoring essays

3 (D)   These essays attempt to answer the question but do so inaccurately or ineffectively. They do not present a clear argument, may not answer the entire question, or are so poorly organized or written that deficiencies interfere with communication. References to the text are likely to be unexplained or vague. Numerous errors in grammar, diction, or syntax will be obvious.

2–1 (F)   These essays compound the weakness of 3–4 papers to the degree that the argument no longer adequately addresses the question or that the paper is close to unreadable. The writer will be unable to make a clear point because of numerous and distracting errors in usage, organization, and clarity. They are often unacceptably brief.

Zero Tolerance Grading

A note: This method addresses revision mainly at the mechanical level.

The English teachers at my school tried an experiment a few years ago—a grading policy called Zero Tolerance, although it might more accurately be called Limited Tolerance, since it allows students to make three mistakes. The idea behind the system is that upper-level high school students *should* know how to avoid common errors, from punctuation glitches and sentence fragments to problems of argumentation. My colleagues were tired of marking the same errors again and again.

The solution: a list for all students (in all English classes) of common errors in papers. After a teacher marked three of these errors on a single paper, he or she would simply draw a line across the paper and stop grading until the student revised. The draft, at that point, received a failing grade, though a rewrite could result in a substantial rise in that grade. The wise student would fix not only the three errors the teacher marked, but also similar errors throughout the rest of the paper, since the teacher would simply hand the paper back with another line a bit further down if those later errors remained.

In practice, the policy worked differently for different teachers. One colleague continues to use the Zero Tolerance rules more or less as I've described, demanding that students complete revision after revision until the errors are gone (sometimes this results in students who are still working on revisions of a first essay and first drafts of a second essay at the same time, since the rest of the class moves on). Other teachers have modified the policy in various ways, using the list as a guideline for revision or grading. Teachers in lower grades hand the students the entire list but tell them they're not responsible for all items on it, or that they will stop grading the paper after, say, six errors. Some teachers interpret the rules to mean that marking halts after three *different* errors have occurred, while others stop after any three errors, even if they're the same type. Most teachers do not apply the rules to in-class or timed writing.

The benefit, regardless of individual interpretation, is that students see a common set of ultimate expectations for writing no matter the class or grade. Parents, too, know that all students in all grades are expected to be working toward error-free papers.

Here's the list of Zero Tolerance errors from my school:

1. Run-on sentences or fragments
2. A lack of uniform or sophisticated style in a paragraph, including too many simple sentences, lack of flow or transition from one sentence or paragraph to another, or awkward or incorrect syntax

3. Too much plot summary, especially without sufficient analysis of text

4. Nonparallel structure of words, clauses, or phrases and agreement problems

5. Inconsistent verb tense

6. Improper possessive forms (apostrophe errors)

7. Comma and semicolon errors

8. "Hanging" quotations (quotations from the text that are not smoothly and grammatically worked into a sentence explaining the relevance of the quotation and, preferably, suggesting some analytical purpose)

9. Incorrect formatting of quotations, including citation format and style/usage errors

10. Use of passive voice except where it contributes to style

11. Improper use of informal language or argumentation

12. Failure to format the title of a book, play, or story correctly

13. Failure to provide at least two appropriate, quoted words or phrases with an analytical explanation in each body paragraph

14. Failure to organize and address a valid textual issue in the paper as a whole—in other words, failure to write a complete, persuasive, and well-thought-out formal essay

15. Failure to answer the question or essay topic

Publication

A few years ago I announced to an AP English class that their final thesis papers, which they'd worked on for a whole term, would each be read by another faculty member who would then meet with me and the author to discuss the paper. Surprisingly, volunteers came out of the woodwork to read the papers—math teachers, foreign language teachers, administrators, and even parents wanted to participate. I also announced that I would collect the final papers into a book that would be shelved and catalogued in our school library. I've never seen such intent revision take place in a few short days.

Publication takes many forms, from literary journals to bulletin boards. Consider these possibilities:

- Post all final drafts (not necessarily only the "best" papers) on a bulletin board or web site.

- Collect final drafts as exemplars for future students.

- Invite other teachers or parents to become readers. One teacher I know holds a special evening event each year at which parents and grandparents are invited to read student papers and discuss the content with the students.

- Collect one final draft from each student to publish in a book or journal, then give each student a copy of the final anthology.

- Have students prepare their writing for city, state, and national writing contests. Make sure the students are responsible for following all formatting, length, and writing requirements.

- Invite students to read final drafts aloud for the class or for events outside of class.

Whatever the form of publication, be sure to tell students what you're doing and why. Knowing their work will be read by a real audience encourages students to revise. It also gives them better tools for revision, since their voices are now directed toward actual, not hypothetical, readers.

Using Revision Strategies

I've found that each of the strategies presented in this chapter is useful only to a limited degree; students get tired of the same approach in class and want variety. That's fine, since ultimately the goal is to dispense with the strategies entirely, or at least to have each student adopt and use the strategies that fit his or her process and writing best. As long as the goal of every exercise is to improve the quality of writing, any method might work, but several methods in tandem—perhaps in response to multiple writing assignments—might work even better.

5 Can We Leave Yet?

Revising on Demand

You don't say, "I've done it!" You come, with a kind of horrible desperation, to realize that this will do.

—Anthony Burgess

The first time I taught AP English, I spent two nail-biting hours waiting for a couple of dozen juniors to finish the essay portion of the exam. I made a show of grading papers while I waited, but I was preoccupied. Would they write as well as I knew they could? Would they bother to remember anything we'd discussed in class? Even after the bleary-eyed students emerged, I had little confidence that they'd written well, and no way of knowing *what* they'd written.

A few days later the essay prompts themselves were turned over to me. I took a look at a few of the green prompt sheets in surprise; they were covered not only with prewriting outlines and ideas but also with drawings, notes, and comments on the essays. One student wrote me a letter. At the end of it, she'd written, "Don't worry, Mr. G.—I finished the essays twenty minutes ago. I'm just waiting until I can go."

Finished twenty minutes ago? I stared at that paper, dumbfounded. This student had actually taken twenty minutes to write me a letter instead of revising or adding to her essays. And then it dawned on me—what else had I given her to do during that time? Revise? Had we really discussed what that meant?

Ten years later, I don't worry much on the day of the exam. There's no particular zen to it; in part, as time has passed, I've come to see that how the students perform on the exam is only one reflection, and possibly not the best one, of my teaching or their learning in my course as a whole. I enjoy the little doodles on the prompt sheets, but there aren't as many of them now. And, too, I now know that I've done all I can to help students by the time they take the exam itself, including making sure that they don't sit around twiddling their thumbs for twenty minutes after dashing off three mediocre essays.

In short, I give them a revision checklist. Nothing on the list comes at them out of the blue; it's the same approach we've used more casually throughout the year. It's the same approach I've described so far in this book. But this time it's a little different—there's an element of speed involved, and the student must adjust his or her revision process to fit *exactly* the amount of time left in the testing period. One way to do this is to pace the revision; another is to set priorities.

The best way to use the checklist—and this is important—is to follow the steps *in order*. If you've got four minutes left before the end of the exam, I tell students, only complete step one. If you've got half an hour, complete them all, or as many as you can. The order of the list stems from a trade-off: what is most effective balanced against what can be achieved quickly—in timed writing, the student must seek a happy medium.

Advanced students, of course, might undertake several of the tasks on the list at once, especially after practice. I still think a list is a good idea, since it helps writers remember exactly what aspects of the paper to check under stressful circumstances.

First, the short version of the list:

The Ten- (or Twenty-, or Thirty-) Minute Revision: A Checklist

1. Proofread.

2. Revisit verbs.

3. Revisit adjectives.

4. Identify your thesis statement and strengthen it.

5. Identify the most important sentence in your conclusion and strengthen it.

6. Strengthen your introduction overall.

7. Strengthen your conclusion overall.

8. Check your evidence from start to finish.

9. Check your syntax from the outside in.

10. Complicate your argument in the penultimate paragraph.

11. Revisit your nouns.

12. Recopy the entire essay.

Now, some explanation of these steps.

Using the Ten-Minute Revision Checklist

1. Proofread.

I include this step first because it's what we all think to do after writing a first draft. It's tempting, though, to leave this step off entirely, for two reasons:

- Ask students what it means to proofread a timed essay and they'll probably answer like this: "Oh, you know, checking spelling and stuff." What they mean is this: "Checking spelling"—the "stuff" remains pretty vague unless you have a specific plan of attack. But how much good is reading for spelling going to do? Are you much more likely to spell *orangutan* correctly the second time if you missed it the first?

- Readers of timed essays—AP, SAT, standardized test readers, and the like—are more highly trained than students (or teachers) sometimes give them credit for. What's more, they know they're looking at first drafts, and they don't expect perfection. Spelling in this context is a forgivable error; bad thinking is not. Time might be better spent crafting a better explanation of catharsis than trying to spell the term correctly.

Nonetheless, proofreading serves a purpose. For one, it allows the writer to catch any really elementary errors—a word left out, a character wrongly identified. What's more, rereading might spark a new idea or suggest a new phrasing. But the general imperative to "proofread" is no more useful for a timed essay than a prepared one if the word does not connote a full strategy for revision.

2. Revisit verbs.

Because verbs add so much power to sentences and because this can be done quickly, I recommend it as a second step. Encourage students to arm themselves with a few interesting and specific verbs. Even when I've spent a full year exhorting students to fill up their mental barrels of verbs, I also suggest keeping a select few right at the top for quick insertion into an essay.

3. Revisit adjectives.

Again, a trip to the barrel is a quick and effective way to improve an interpretative paper. The idea here is to scan the essay quickly for culprits such as the words *tone*, *attitude*, or *mood* and to add specificity to the discussion of such literary elements through well-placed modifiers.

4. Identify your thesis statement and strengthen it.

I place this item fourth assuming that most students, having practiced for a timed test, will fashion a decent working thesis in the first place. But the statement—or statements—in which the core idea of the argument is expressed might just benefit from a second look. This is a good time to remember the barrels of syntactical and rhetorical constructions, since these models may not only improve the flow of the thesis, they may actually help with the clarity of how a writer expresses central points.

5. Identify the most important sentence in your conclusion and strengthen it.

The final summation of the argument is likewise a key target. Readers not only put the essay down with the final paragraph resonating in their heads, they actually often *look* for the strengths or weaknesses of the conclusion when considering nudging a score up or down. A powerful restatement or summary of ideas can save an argument that seems to be wilting near the end.

6. Strengthen your introduction overall.

Many writers of on-demand essays use a one-sentence introduction. The sentence serves as a springboard into the argument itself—the reader notices the introduction, sees that it's on point, and moves on to the second paragraph to determine the overall value of the essay.

Personally, I only recommend the one-sentence approach to students who have trouble finishing an assignment in the allotted time (it also works in disciplines besides English—an AP history essay, for instance, might not benefit from a long introduction). For those who write more quickly, I suggest working on the introduction up front—I believe that if you can sell your reader on the power of the argument and of your writing in the first paragraph, why wait? A caveat, though: this takes practice. Most students *don't* write strong introductions naturally. Most restate the prompt, wallow in generalities, and wind up repeating a fairly simple thesis several times. But a sophisticated introduction that gives a solid overview of the analytical procedure to come can serve as a foundation for the rest of the essay.

When students do take the one-sentence approach, I suggest that, given time, it's worthwhile to rewrite the entire introduction before rewriting any other section of the essay. If it doesn't work, one can always cross out the new version and stick with the original. For students who tend to ramble in the introduction, this might be a good time to check for generalizations and lame repetitions of the prompt that loosen the whole paragraph.

7. Strengthen your conclusion overall.

After the introduction, the conclusion. Same rules apply: get rid of generalizations, increase the sophistication and clarity of ideas and how they are expressed.

8. Check your evidence from start to finish.

Almost every rubric for an interpretive on-demand essay includes the phrase "ample and appropriate evidence" in the description of high-scoring papers. The reason is simple: the more evidence a writer discusses, the deeper the analysis might go. Have students check evidence paragraph by paragraph. Is there enough? Are there important phrases that didn't make it into the first draft? Is evidence taken equally from the beginning, middle, and end of the passage?

9. Check your syntax from the outside in.

One could take a paragraph-by-paragraph approach to revising for syntax, as well, but I prefer to work from the beginning and end of the essay toward the middle. Have students check the introduction and conclusion first to be sure that ideas are well-phrased and that the syntax works to the advantage of those ideas. Then check the start of the second paragraph and the end of the penultimate paragraph and work inward from there. The middle of an essay can stand to be more prosaic in its style than the opening and closing sections, which often profess more complicated ideas and thus benefit more from carefully honed sentence structure.

This is a good time, too, to try a little sentence combining. Are there simple sentences that can be connected by a semicolon, and if so, can a quick change of a verb or noun make the two clauses parallel? Are there sentences that would benefit from a dependent clause?

10. Complicate your argument in the penultimate paragraph.

Generally speaking, the second to last paragraph of an essay includes the most important pieces of the argument. In an interpretative essay, this is where the end of the passage or poem is usually discussed; whether the author ended the passage naturally at this point or the creators of the test chose to end an excerpt at this point, the ending is important. Good questions for students to ask: have I really done justice to *all* of the ideas expressed in the ending? Are there lingering questions? Are there tie-ins to the introduction that I've missed? Can I somehow recognize any other subtleties or nuances of the argument or stylistic connections?

In a non-interpretive, personal essay, some of the same questions apply. The penultimate paragraph may well contain the climax of a story or an epiphany. Again, have students ask themselves if there are lingering questions, subtleties or uncertainties of meaning, or ideas that still need to be expressed.

11. Revisit your nouns.

In a timed essay, nouns tend to get replaced by quoted passages of text to be good enough to do the job. Nonetheless, it's worth a quick search for any vague labels such as "thing" or the overused "etc." Specificity is the goal here—are the nouns as specific and interesting as possible?

12. Recopy the entire essay.

It happens; students finish the essay, revise as best they can, and still have twenty minutes to stare at the wall. In this case, my advice is simple: recopy the whole essay. Every word. Why? For one thing, it's something to do. For another, it's a chance to improve handwriting, to get rid of crossed out words, and generally to offer a better visual presentation.

But the real reason is more important. Recopying forces a writer to slow down, reconsider, and reshape prose. Phrases that may never have given the author pause during rereading may stand out glaringly when the writer has to copy over every letter. It's a rare case in which there's time for this step, but when there is, the essay invariably is the better for it.

The entire checklist, of course, is just a series of suggestions. Tailor it to the needs of your students or offer it as a starting place for students to construct their own strategies and revision priorities. You might also try some of the following ideas in preparation for timed writing assessments:

- Practice revision using the checklist. Initially, at least, offer students a separate time to think about revision of timed work. At first, for instance, give students one class period in which to write an assignment and the next in which to revise using the checklist (you can work through the list item by item or just let students follow it at their own pace). Then, gradually shorten the time you allow for revision to thirty minutes, then twenty, then ten, then five.

- Use a variety of samples for revision. It's profitable, of course, for students to revise their own work, but utilize other resources as well. Sample high-, medium-, and low-scoring essays from actual AP students are available from the College Board's web site, for instance—any of these might make an interesting focus for a revision exercise. Given a medium-scoring essay written by another student and fifteen minutes, can your class produce a work worthy of a higher score? What's the most efficient way to do so?

- Use metacognition to reflect on the timed revision process. At the end of each exercise, have students consider what worked, what didn't, and how their personal checklists might be refined, reorganized, or reworded for maximum success.

- Try just the final step of my checklist: recopying. Force students to recopy, by hand, an on-demand writing assignment, with the allowance that they may change anything they wish. See what happens and discuss the results in class. How much did they change and what kinds of changes were they? Did they see the essay differently? Might this work best with just one part of the essay, and if so, which one?

- Use technology. I sometimes have seniors type an on-demand assignment or two early in the year just to see the difference. Those who can type well often write much more than they would by hand; others actually change the kinds of sentences they write, their diction, or, if nothing else, their spelling. Most writing assessments don't offer the option of typing responses, so I pretty quickly move to handwritten essays in class, but the initial typed essays may prove to students what they're capable of producing in a short period of time given the resources.

  Technology is very useful for revision, as well. In general, one can practice reorganization, identify repeated structures and words, and keep track of multiple revisions easily using a word processing program. You might also try having students type on-demand assignments that were initially handwritten and discussing the kinds of changes and the quality of those changes—were they similar to or different from those one might make when recopying by hand?

- Practice possible ways of preparing for revision while writing the first draft. At the least, have students skip lines in their essays to leave room for possible revision of words, phrases, or sentences. You might also discuss other ways of leaving room for revision: leaving enough space to rewrite a whole paragraph, writing one paragraph per page so that one might cross out the first attempt and recopy it below, or leaving room to rewrite a single sentence if time permits. Readers are used to arrows, insertions, and crossed-out passages and are willing to work with students, but students are more likely to revise if the physical space on the page invites it.

Knowing the Test (and the Readers)

Before I started teaching, I worked for two years for a major testing company, first as a reader of on-demand writing and then as a table leader (a reader who also oversees several other readers and helps to train new readers). The great frustration of the job was that I felt so removed from the student writers. There we'd sit, forty or fifty readers divided into small groups of six or eight, reading piles of essays, discussing what the students did well and what we wished we could tell them. At times we'd share a particularly well-written essay aloud; at other times we'd share our frustration when a student seemed to fall just short of the mark. And what I never lost as a reader, in all of that time, was my desire to write on the essays, to give comments back to students, to help them revise a piece.

One way to help students prepare to revise on-demand writing is to talk with them about the test, the readers, and the process. Tests are systematic and readers are trained to work as a team, but readers are also human. A student who writes furiously for thirty minutes in a timed setting may be able to relax and think about his or her audience for a final ten minutes—and to revise appropriately. A few hints:

- Teach students how the test is scored. Students can think beyond the English classroom, here. Many writing assessments are scored holistically, but in some AP subjects, for instance, it's not necessary to have a thesis statement or even a full, formal essay—a series of paragraphs might do the trick. Stylistic sophistication on such tests counts only insofar as it aids in the communication of ideas; on the AP English exam or SAT writing portion, on the other hand, stylistic flair is an important element of high-scoring responses.

- Have students study rubrics (and make their own). Part of learning how a test is scored involves familiarizing students with the scoring scale and rubrics. Look especially at items common to many sample rubrics for a particular assessment.

- Know what readers want to see and know what they *don't* hold against students. You can glean a lot about the mindset of readers from the numerous resources many testing companies provide: reader responses to specific prompts, teacher workshops, test guides, and preparation resources. Even better, you can find and talk to an actual person who has scored an AP or SAT writing portion, or even better than that, you can contact the College Board or other testing organizations about becoming a scorer yourself—there's no better way to learn what readers want to see than to become one.

  However, there's one more pretty good way to get an idea of what readers tire of and what excites them—read a whole lot of on-demand essays. As a teacher, you know the mistakes your students make as a whole, but do they? Try having students read and score not just an essay or two but dozens—keep both the authors and scorers anonymous. You might, in fact, set up your room like a professional scoring center, with a small number of students at each table reading a stack of essays—assign a table leader to review the rubric, practice scoring sample essays, and read behind other readers to check on score accuracy. Consider slipping in a few samples by students from a previous year or from the samples provided by the testing service to keep students on their toes or to add variety to the scores.

  Once students have read, say, fifty or sixty essays each, discuss the process and what they've learned about what readers do or don't want to see. Ask if they'll approach writing or revising on demand any differently.

  So what do readers of on-demand writing want to see? First of all, let's consider what most assessments claim they *don't* count against students:

- poor handwriting

- poor spelling, unless it interferes with comprehension

- scribbles, cross-outs, erasures, arrows with insertions

- some organizational issues (I've heard AP readers discuss the concept of *internal paragraphing*, in which transitions occur but without indenting a sentence on a new line)

It's true that flaws in papers such as these are forgivable and might be overlooked in assigning a score to a paper; it's just as true that a paper that's easy to read predisposes a scorer to look on it kindly, or at least doesn't predispose a scorer to judge the paper harshly. In other words, poor handwriting might not hurt a paper, but it certainly can't *help*. If students consistently have trouble with any of these "forgivable" areas, it might be worth targeting those areas during the few minutes the students have to polish and revise—check handwriting, look for places to mark paragraph breaks, recopy a sentence that's troublesome to read.

As for what readers *do* want to see, here are a few thoughts:

- A response that shows an awareness of *all* aspects of the prompt and that does everything the prompt asks
- An introduction that is engaging and does not simply restate the prompt
- Explanations of how and why devices, structures, and aspects of style are used (not simply an awareness that they exist)
- Fresh approaches, organic development, natural style
- A complete essay (no excuses, for instance, about running out of time)
- Clear transitions and organization

Replicating On-Demand Testing in Your School

Let's begin this discussion with a basic supposition: on-demand writing involves a skill set similar, but not identical, to prepared essay writing. Specifically, the revision process for each type of writing is distinct, as is the process of organizing and prewriting. Consider, for example, a student I taught several years ago—let's call him Joseph.

Joseph was no natural writer, but he did what too few students do: he took advantage of the resources available to him. I'd assign an essay a week or so in advance of the due date, and that afternoon Joseph would appear in my room to discuss his topic. I specifically recall letting students choose their own topics for a paper on *Heart of Darkness*—Joseph came to me with the fairly basic idea of writing about the Congo River as a symbol, but he didn't have much more to work with. Together, he and I drew a little map of the river, labeling Marlow's three major stops and outlining some possibly symbolic incidents that take place at each. Then, I simply wrote numbers above the three stops on our map: one, two, three.

"Hey," Joseph said. "I could write a paragraph about each one, couldn't I?"

My first mental response, I admit it, was this:

Duh.

My second (and more professional) mental response was relief that Joseph was getting it. Sure, he was going to produce a pretty straightforward five-paragraph essay, but at that point, I'd count a strong five-paragraph essay from Joseph a victory. Sure enough, he appeared in my room the *next* afternoon with an outline, and the day after that, with a rough draft. By the time the final draft arrived on my desk the next week, the paper deserved a high B, largely because Joseph put in the time planning and revising *before* the assignment was due. And he got better—later papers took less time on my part and were just as good, because Joseph figured out the process.

Nice success story, you're thinking. *So what?*

A success, yes. Except for one thing: when it was time to write an on-demand essay, Joseph failed miserably. If he even got farther along than the prewriting stage in the allotted time, his hasty attempts at constructing a logical essay came out something like a verbal version of the jungle in Conrad's novel; I found myself looking at the tangle of illogical sentences and whispering, "The horror . . . the horror . . ."

Joseph was never going to take the AP English exam, and he barely missed taking the writing portion of the SAT, but there was a bigger concern looming on the horizon, and he knew it: college exams. He'd visited the college of his choice, sat in on classes, seen the syllabi, and he knew what was coming. He would have to write essays.

For most students, it's more important in the long run to learn to utilize resources—to get an editor, to plan writing in advance, to revise strategically. I can't think of a single time since I left school that I've had to submit a first draft of anything—I always have time to rewrite, to edit, to revise. But I've gotten behind on deadlines and written in a rush, and that's when the skills of the on-demand writer kick in. And as long as students remain in school, they'll face on-demand assignments.

Joseph learned to write prepared essays by practicing. Students have to practice on-demand writing, too. They have to practice revising timed writing. Many of them, unfortunately, never get that practice unless they take an AP class.

Joseph wasn't alone—many of the seniors I taught were unprepared for timed writing assignments. When I discussed the situation with my colleagues, it was our tenth grade English teacher who came up with the solution: more preparation. That year, we instituted a new program, a school-wide timed writing assessment given at the beginning and end of every school year to *every* high school student. The essays, identified only by a number assigned to each student, are then scored on a nine-point holistic scale by two different teachers, with discrepancies being decided by a third reader.

Are you serious?

Well, yes. However, I teach in a small high school, with few English teachers—at most, we read about two hundred essays as a group, and we don't make comments on them. We meet after school every day for about a week and read the essays together, and the benefits are numerous:

- The students get to practice, at least twice per year, not just writing a timed essay but trying to match the blindly scored result to the rubric

- The teachers get to discuss essay writing and how we teach it—invariably, the exercise results in a conversation about which of us should teach, say, citation format or smoother incorporation of evidence

- The teachers also get to see the stages of student writing throughout high school—as one who teaches mostly seniors, it's of great benefit to me to be reminded of how underclassmen write

- We can track the progress of our students as a whole, compare classes, and identify weaknesses at the start of the year

Sounds great, but what if your school had two thousand students and twenty English teachers?

Unless you have an unusually unified and committed department, I wouldn't try a schoolwide on-demand assignment. You might, however, try combining forces with a few other teachers, especially if you can include teachers who work with multiple grade levels. You could team up with a history teacher or one from another discipline. Anything you can do to increase the practice your students have at writing on demand serves to increase the chances that your students will improve at the skill of timed writing.

The process is simple. First, we agree on a prompt, usually one adapted from an actual AP exam. For our purposes, we use the "open-ended" format, in which students choose any work of literature (in the fall, for instance, each student writes about one of his or her summer reading assignments) and answer an open-ended question. You could, however, have students interpret a passage or write a persuasive or personal essay. Here are a few examples of recent prompts from my school:

- Many people who have written about tragedy refer to the hero's or heroine's tragic flaw. This flaw may take many forms—pride, lust for power, the inability to see circumstances as they really are—but in every case, the flaw somehow contributes to the ultimate downfall of the character. Choose a novel or play you have read this year that might be considered a tragedy. In a formal essay, discuss the nature of the protagonist's flaw, how that flaw contributes to the protagonist's downfall, and how the character's flaw affects the tragic nature and meaning of the work as a whole. Avoid plot summary.

- In many works of literature, characters reveal psychological depth and development to the reader unwittingly. Choose a novel, play, or epic poem in which the reader, through insight and inference, gains a deeper understanding of a character's psyche than that character has himself. In a well-organized essay, discuss the ways in which the author manages to create the distinction between the character's self-understanding and the reader's understanding of the character.

- The medieval writer Sebastian Brant (1458–1521) wrote, "The world wants to be deceived." In a well-organized essay, discuss this statement as it applies to a work of literary merit you have read for your English class. In your essay, address the types of deception that exist in the work (you may discuss acts of deception by the characters, the author, or both) and how that deception is necessary for the overall meaning of the work to be comprehended.

These prompts, of course, are meant to imitate those on the AP exam. I've known middle school teachers to use simpler versions:

- *Romeo and Juliet* is a play in which many characters think of love differently. Choose three characters and discuss how each thinks about the nature of love. Then discuss the message about love you think Shakespeare meant us to take away from this play.
- Choose one work you read this year and write an essay about the conflicts faced by the main character. In the first body paragraph, describe the conflict. In the second body paragraph, discuss how the character overcomes the conflict (or fails to overcome it). In the final body paragraph, discuss how that conflict relates to an overall theme of the work.

Once the students write the essays, our teachers gather after school every day for about a week to read the essays. The first day goes slowly; we attune ourselves to a general rubric, read a few sample essays, and discuss the nature of the assignment. Then we get down to business, rapidly reading and scoring each essay without commentary. At the end of the week, we compile the scores by class and grade and examine them together. Are the scores what we'd expect? Do we see any particular weaknesses? Are our students improving as writers of on-demand assignments overall?

There's a unique sense of perspective to be gained from reading essays with other teachers; the discussion raises issues, ideas for teaching, and concerns that you might never notice yourself. It's also nice to feel you're not alone—after all, I sometimes feel that I've taken on as my job the task of teaching what I love (writing) but surrounded myself with writing done poorly. Misery, as I said earlier, loves company—perhaps because misery can be negated by it to some extent.

Possibilities for Revision

To our purpose: don't neglect the possibilities for revision that writing on demand not only offers but, well, demands. Since I regularly ask students to write timed assignments for my AP classes, I use a fair number of follow-up and revision exercises; other teachers in my school have students revise the on-demand assignments they write each fall and spring until they are polished products. Again, a student who sees what he or she is capable of producing given time might just be more likely to produce a better product within a limited period.

Some ideas for revising students' timed essays:

- Before revising their own essays, ask students to make a scoring rubric, pick exemplars (sample high-, medium- and low-scoring essays) from an anonymous group of papers, or reflect on the prompt itself—what possible answers might one expect, and what possible flaws?

- Another pre-revision idea: have students grade some of the essays themselves. I sometimes ask each student to read, say, five or six essays (again, all names are removed from the papers) and score each using my rubric. When each essay has been scored several times, the scores are returned to the author. If I use these scores for a grade, I average the scores together but drop the lowest score; I also read all of the essays myself to be sure the student scores are in the ballpark.

- If, in fact, it's possible for multiple classes to use the same prompt, switch papers with students from another class (anonymously or not). Try peer-editing across classes, grades, or disciplines; set ground rules about the types of comments to be made if necessary. Better yet, encourage discussion about the prompt and how students approached it between students from different classes and grades (technology can help with this—comments can be posted online for all students to see; I've even tried similar activities between schools in different cities).

- Try putting the essays aside for a few weeks, until after the students have done some other writing and thinking about writing. Then let them come back and revise with fresh eyes, and discuss the results.

- If all your students receive on a timed assignment is a holistic score, ask them to figure out the rationale behind the score and explain it. Do this in peer groups or as a homework assignment; either way, try to get students to look at the paper objectively, as an outside reader would.

- Use the same prompt later in the year after you've taught some other works of literature. Then have students choose the better of the two essays, revise it, and submit it for the only grade—for the other essay, offer no grade or a minor completion grade. Discuss the role of the work one chooses as a topic in determining the quality of the essay, the author's desire to write and revise, and the ease of revision.

- Revise the essays using a pass-around activity. Have students sit in a circle; each student passes his or her essay (again, make them anonymous if you wish) around the circle. The rule: each person makes one new comment, suggestion, or correction on each essay—one and only one. By the time the paper gets back to the author, there will be as many comments as there are students in the class, and each student will have read all of the essays (you can try this in smaller groups and stipulate one comment per paragraph if you wish). Then have students revise their essays using these comments. Don't forget to get into the circle yourself.

On-demand writing is tricky but important, and every student is likely to encounter some type of timed assignment during his or her educational career. It's worth spending some time helping students devise a strategy for such assignments. Who knows? They might even thank you—possibly in a letter scrawled in the margins of the prompt sheet from an AP exam.

6 *You're Just My Type*

Revising with Technology

I must admit that it is a help in self-criticism. Typescript is so impersonal and hideous to look at, if I type out a poem, I immediately see defects which I missed in looking through it in manuscript.
—W. H. Auden

Writers and English teachers are a notoriously hide-bound bunch. I know English teachers who still look with some skepticism at the mechanical pencil, and I sometimes feel like joining their ranks. In high school, when I wrote a great deal of mediocre poetry (or perhaps that's flattering myself), computers were still monstrous things that projected green letters on black screens; I learned to write from my high school teacher, Bill Brown, by tucking a notebook and pen into my backpack and heading to a window at our downtown school from which I could see the world. Now I write on a laptop computer; it's a bit more advanced than, say, the clay tablets Catullus wrote on with a stylus and then rubbed with pumice. But writing habits aren't entirely defined by technology (I still haul my laptop off to coffee shops and picnic tables to write), and writing itself doesn't have to be, either.

Students will always be quicker than most teachers to embrace technology, but many English teachers today see the value of technology as a tool for learning and revision. In fact, say what you will about the writing process, word processing is now essential to the publication process, and I'd argue it's one of a writing teacher's most valuable tools. Aspects of revision that drove previous generations crazy, such as retyping or rewriting, literally, an entire composition, are now easier than ever. So easy, perhaps, that students sometimes see their work as lamentably expendable (no one used to toss out an essay with teacher comments on it easily, I bet, when they were written with hard-earned peacock quills on lambskin parchment).

This chapter includes ideas and strategies for using technology to help and encourage students to revise what they write. The idea behind these suggestions, though, is to increase efficiency and student interest in the process, not to replace the creative work that goes into revision with an automated process. Like those teachers who look askance at the mechanical pencil, I'm still skeptical of machine-scoring essays, grammar checks on word processors, and any other technology that removes rather than assists the human element of writing and reconsidering what we write. Time may prove me wrong, I suppose, and I may seem as much a Luddite as Eeyore, whom I recall from childhood condemning the whole practice altogether: "This writing business," he said. "Pencils and what-not. Over-rated, if you ask me. Silly stuff. Nothing in it."

But my computer's automatic grammar check says Eeyore's syntax needs correction, and the spell-check doesn't think his name is a real word. Shows what it knows. There's still a necessity for human creativity in the process of polishing work, but perhaps technology can give that creativity a boost just when students need it the most.

TOOLS OF THE TRADE: *Using the Machines We Have*

Let's begin with what may seem like science fiction for some classrooms today and in several years may sound hopelessly dated. Imagine this: a student hand-writes an assignment. The composition is edited, color-coded, and corrected with the help of several other students and the teacher, then it's published and read by a class in, say, New York. Here's the kicker: it all happens without any-one using *a single sheet of paper*. Here's the next kicker: the author lives in a vil-lage in Thailand where there's no electricity.

Technology is changing so fast that writing about tools seems almost hope-less. I've recently seen prototypes of computers built into clothing, cell phones that fit on the finger like a thimble, and laptops powered by hand cranks for use in less developed nations, including Thailand. I'm writing this chapter on a tablet PC; I can flip the screen around, lay it flat against the keyboard, and write directly onto it with a stylus—the computer converts my handwriting to text.

But look: our students still need to learn to write, to revise, to think, to read. I still like real books, and voices, and to see students whose faces aren't bathed in the glow of an LCD screen. Quite often, students and I work through several drafts of a paper without ever printing a hard copy of the essay; at other times, I want students writing poems in marker on poster paper just to get them to release their inhibitions. Technology breaks down when you need it most, it's a distraction for some students, and sometimes you just want a paper to be turned in on, well, paper—but when it works, it really works. And one's strategies, I've found, depend largely upon the technology one has at hand. With that in mind, consider some possibilities for using technological devices that you may have access to now or in the near future:

- With a PC projector, you can project a poem, student essay, or assign-ment on a screen or wall. How this helps with revision: it's a great way to model practices for students. I project paragraphs onto the dry erase board in my room and make corrections and edit and color code in dry erase marker. I used to combine the projector with a smart board in my classroom to make the process more efficient (the smart board could capture what I wrote and translate it to digital markings), but:

- I now use a tablet PC. The tablet allows me to write directly onto my laptop rather than onto the board. I might, for instance, project a paragraph, then make edits directly on my laptop (projected for the class to see). The real benefit is that I can then save these "handwritten" marks and email the file to students, who can then use the text with my comments for review. I also comment on student papers this way at times, though since I type faster than I write I just often add my comments to electronic papers by typing them.

- Laptop computers, which schools are now buying in greater numbers than desktop computers, offer teachers the ability to group students in a variety of ways, to use the computer, close it, then open it again easily, and to individualize instruction by arranging the physical space between students and the teacher.

- Email has revolutionized the way I teach. Though email carries its own dangers, including oversight for appropriate content and modes of discourse (ever read a student email that seems more like an e. e. cummings poem than a formal letter to a teacher?), the benefits for revision are numerous. It's not just that students can hand in papers electronically; email provides a means for conversing about papers that just didn't exist before. I still talk with students in person all the time, but I also discuss topics, answer quick questions, make suggestions, and return comments by email. Email is especially handy for long-term projects and with students who are shy about coming by in person to ask a question or seek help.

- Consider using online discussion forums, instant messaging, and chat rooms for student group work. All of these uses of technology require teacher oversight and organization, but imagine the possibilities:

  - Each student posts a paragraph on a discussion forum (there are plenty of free hosts online; you can find them just by searching for free discussion forums)

  - For each paragraph, a group of students responds with suggestions and comments

  - The author then has a chance to ask questions of the group or submit a revision

  - The group then responds once more

Benefits of this approach: it doesn't take up a minute of class time, the students can complete the assignment at their leisure, and there's a record of everything the group does for the teacher to review.

- Programs that machine-score student essays have received a fair bit of criticism, but software companies continue to refine and produce these programs. In a world of high-stakes testing, such assistants to over-worked teachers may well become not just more common, but more useful. I'm not sold on any of these programs yet; anecdotal evidence that, for instance, quantity sometimes matters more than quality to such programs keeps me skeptical. However, machine-scoring might be useful for revision in that it allows a first draft to be graded quickly and impersonally and helps students get to the point of revision more quickly. For some students, such scoring might also catch weaknesses a teacher misses (we're all human, after all) or, better yet, reinforce a point a teacher has been trying to make (because often humans get it right).

As you consider possible group collaboration techniques online, keep in mind some of the differences between types of collaboration—all of these formats, by the way, have become extremely easy to create and use through free online hosts.

- Chat rooms are instant messaging sessions that are useful for informal, real-time conversations (with the option of a printed record).

- Forums and bulletin boards allow teachers to pose a set question, prompt, or text for analysis and gather organized student responses over time.

- Blogs are personal pages that can include responses from others. Blogs are essentially a form of personal publication; pages usually have a personalized look and feel.

- Wikis are pages that allow small groups of people to collaborate and create a document together. They can be useful for group work and creating communal class notes, for instance, but they are also open to vandalism by users other than the creator of the wiki.

- Online rubrics, if you use rubrics, are available from a number of sources. I've also known teachers to create simple rubrics in a spreadsheet that tabulate grades for them, assigning a particular weight to a comment such as "good," "excellent," or "needs work" and using those weights to produce a final grade.

There's no telling what technology will come along in the near future that will once again reshape the way we think of instruction, but so far, most of these tools are just that—tools. They don't replace the kind of revision writers have been using all along; in many ways they're just a continuation of the assistance for revision that came along first from erasers, Wite-Out, and correctable typewriter ribbons. A difference, though, is that computers have reshaped how we arrange classrooms, instruction time, and our interaction with students. They can also help reshape student attitudes toward writing and revision—below are some suggestions that might help in this area.

Individual Revision Strategies

To begin with, here's how students and I typically work together to revise electronically:

- The student types a paper and emails it to me. I save the paper on my computer.

- I use features of my word processing program to comment on and edit the paper:

  - First and foremost, I choose Track Changes (in Microsoft Word, you'll find this option under the Tools menu or by pressing the Control, Shift, and E buttons at once). Once I choose Track Changes, <u>anything I type shows up underlined</u> (and, on my screen, in color). The student can keep what I type or erase it.

  - I sometimes highlight text in various colors to help students match it to my comments or to point out repetitions and errors.

  - Using the AutoText option under AutoCorrect in the Tools menu, I set up standard comments that can be inserted to save me time. For instance, when I type *inqt* on my keyboard, Word automatically replaces those characters with this: "<u>You could really integrate this quotation into the paper more smoothly</u>."

  - I might go to the Insert menu and choose to insert a Comment. This way I can type in a comment that appears only when the student holds the mouse above the word or phrase I've chosen.

  - With my tablet PC, I can choose simply to write comments directly onto the screen and save them as part of the document. Remember Maria's paragraph from Chapter 2? Figure 6–1 shows comments I made on Maria's paragraph with my tablet PC.

- Other students also read the paper and comment on it in similar ways. If another student has already tracked changes on the essay before I get it, my comments show up in a different color so that the author can tell what each reader wrote.

- I email the paper back to the student, who revises and emails it back to me, and so on.

Some software companies now produce products specifically tailored to writing teachers that feature preset comments or the possibility of sending

COMBINE?

In William Shakespeare's play *Romeo and Juliet,* the two main characters,

Romeo and Juliet, seem to fall in love at first sight. Throughout the play,

issues of love are addressed by many characters. By examining the scene

BEST CHOICE?

in which the two characters meet, the balcony scene, and Juliet's first

meeting with Paris, it can be proven that it is possible for characters in

SPLIT INF.

Romeo and Juliet to truly fall in love at first sight.

Figure 6–1

essays back in web format. I like the ongoing process of revision that working in Word offers.

From the student's end, there are a few more revision tools available through a word processing program:

- The screen can be split between two or more documents so that a student can look at an original document or a page of comments and the revision at the same time (just open two documents in Word and use the Window menu to "split").

- The student can use textboxes to insert metacognitive comments explaining or considering how a piece was written (text boxes can be found under the Insert menu).

- The AutoSummarize option in Word (found under Tools) attempts to highlight a student's key points—it's a difficult and inaccurate task for a computer, but it might help a student reconsider whether or not, in fact, the key points are clear.

- The ability to count words specifically makes cutting exercises easy—just lower the word limit on an essay or story and see what happens. Does the student tighten the writing or lose valuable information when he or she is required to cut one hundred words?

- The ability to cut, copy, and paste text (under the Edit menu) allows students to try switching sentences and paragraphs around without committing to the changes.

- The ability to highlight text in a variety of colors can help students to reconsider all of the verbs, adjectives, and punctuation in a piece at the same time.

- Spell-check options are useful; grammar checks are usually not. A thesaurus built into a word processing program is a nice perk—it often serves up alternatives for redundancies and overly simple diction.

Combining these methods with the ability to share work online quickly and easily and the ability to save multiple versions of the same document has resulted in a new attitude toward revision for many students. It's no longer the onerous task it once was, even if it's not always fun.

Publication and Audience

In Chapter 2 of this book, I discussed the need for an awareness of audience in determining the direction of writing and revision; in Chapter 4, I discussed publication. The Internet provides an opportunity for publication and for an audience, but it's a wide open field with few limits on its content. Websites, wikis, and blogs all offer ways for students to post work and for that work to be read by the school community, including parents, other students, and faculty members. Again, oversight is important here, as it is with any school publication. A conversation in the classroom about appropriate communication can go a long way toward stemming off inappropriate use.

Consider some of the following options for student publication:

- Create student "eportfolios" that include student work of various types. You can have students create a home page on a website or blog that links to various compositions; you might also ask students to create hyperlinks that connect ideas within pieces or redirect readers to an external site relevant to the content of a piece. Set a time for parents to view the eportfolios and return positive comments to the students, or assign students to review one another's portfolios.

- Issue one installment of your school literary magazine online. Choose students as editors and oversee the project as you would a printed literary magazine—you'll save money.

- Use a wiki to create a class novel, research paper, or book of poetry. Some wikis provided by free sites offer templates, password protection, easy tutorials, and limits on who can access the pages. Using hyperlinks, you can also create "choose your own adventure" style stories in which the reader gets to choose options and leaps automatically to the relevant section of the story upon choosing.

- Showcase pieces by students—a poem or essay of the week, for instance—on a website of your own. Make it available to your entire school community and include a photo and brief bio of the student. Allow the student to offer a brief comment on the piece or the assignment from which the writing originated.

- Use a digital camera, video camera, or audio recorder to capture students reading their original work. Then play the recording or show the pictures to other classes during the day—you might also make these recordings available online.

There are as many ways to present student work to an audience as there are types of technology, and in almost every case this type of publication is free. Students can help with setting up sites and with technological problems—heck, they're probably already doing just about anything you or I can think of.

Digital Literacy

Those of us who were educated in the dark ages know what information looks like: a magazine article, a newspaper article, an encyclopedia entry. If you want to find out how something works, you've got to know the Dewey Decimal System, right?

Yeah, right. Dream on.

You know it too: students explore the five or so exabytes (Don't know what an exabyte is? Just think of an amount of information about the size of five thousand Libraries of Congress.) of information added each year to Internet through a search engine and come up with—well, one can only hope they come up with something relatively legitimate and reasonable.

In teaching writing and revision, we shouldn't forget that students who learn to read and write online—to create websites or blogs, for instance—need to learn revision skills for digital communication, as well. Among these skills:

- Writing in smaller phrases and pieces of information that can be read on the screen

- Considering the arrangement of material on the screen as opposed to the page, including the effectiveness of visual material combined with language

- Checking the legitimacy of source material and links and learning to cite accurately

- Writing for an audience that may be both specific and general at the same time—for both those who visit a site intentionally and for surfers

- Learning the skills necessary to create pages, links, and other online publications

I don't want to stop teaching Shakespeare in order to teach digital literacy myself, but I can incorporate these skills in my teaching of *Hamlet* using many of the techniques discussed in this chapter. Other teachers may wish to incorporate entire units on digital literacy, especially in the middle school or early high school years. No matter how or where the information is included, it's an important part of teaching overall literacy, I believe, and will become increasingly so.

Computers and technology in general, in fact, are not going away any time soon. English teachers have the choice either to embrace such technology or to fight against it, and sometimes both approaches are merited. I look for ways to combine technology with the practices I already implement in classes rather than replacing what I do with technology just for its own sake. Discussion still happens in a circle in my classroom; it also happens online. Students still work with partners; they also email one another. I still hand literary magazines to smiling parents; I also post pictures of classroom activities on my website. There's a balance involved, one I'm always seeking to maintain. And if I do it right, it won't be only the revision process that will improve for students, but the entire experience of learning about literature and writing.

7 So, What's Your Story?

Revising Creative Writing

I said, "A line will take us hours maybe,
Yet if it does not seem a moment's thought
Our stitching and unstitching has been naught."
—W. B. Yeats

I recently heard Ted Kooser, who was poet laureate of the United States from 2004 to 2006, say that he revises each of his short poems around thirty or forty times. Hemingway wrote around thirty drafts of some stories, revising on a typewriter. Some authors, like Raymond Carver, revise stories even *after* they've been published. With fiction and poetry, it seems, the number of revisions can be infinite. At what point, after all, does one have to stop revising?

When you die?

Okay, so there's a final rule we can follow: **once you die, it's no longer in draft form**. Before that, all bets are off.

Actually, I'd guess that the world of poets and fiction writers is divided almost neatly in half between those who love to revise, who could do so endlessly, tinkering with endless possibilities and meaning, and those for whom revision feels like mowing the lawn with a pair of nail clippers—tedious and interminable. I'd guess, too, that those from either camp who publish their work regularly learn to revise, and to stop revising, no matter how they feel. Students, I think, usually begin in the latter camp, those who feel like they've written all they have to say the first time around, but become converts to revision as they mature as writers.

Creative writing demands revision. It just does. No one gets the words down in just the right way the first time around with a story or poem. If you think you have, you haven't. Oh, maybe there's an occasional Coleridge who scribbles down "Kubla Kahn" in a delirious rush, but even he needed some time and a suggestion from his buddy Wordsworth before he put an albatross in "Rime of the Ancient Mariner." Students don't always want to believe that creative writing demands revision—the strategies in this chapter ideally convince them not only that individual poems and stories can be improved, but that all poems and stories can.

135

Tips for Revising Creative Writing

Some revision suggestions work for all genres; these instructions are meant to help students revise poetry, fiction, or any kind of creative nonfiction. I don't recommend dumping all of these instructions on students at once—some might be discussed in class, others directed to students once they have a rough draft in front of them. Over time, one hopes students will internalize many of these techniques. With that in mind, here are some of the tips I offer creative writing classes:

- *Give yourself time.* Essays often require quick turn-around times and deadlines. Poems and stories are another matter. Sometimes a poem needs to sit in a drawer for a month or two before you can examine it with fresh eyes. In the meantime, of course, you have to keep writing. Who knows? You may wind up combining poems, writing a better version of one you haven't looked at in a while, or just improving as a writer.

- *Work from a hard copy.* Technology makes it easy to revise on the page, but with poems, the visual is important, and with stories, length makes real paper useful. I suggest printing out a first draft for revision purposes—in fact, I suggest retyping creative works from scratch. It's surprising how much you'll find yourself changing in the process.

- *Revisit the imagery and diction of the piece.* Are images concrete and unique? Are there more specific words available? Could any of the ideas be better supported by physical details or examples? Are the reader's senses engaged?

- *Show, don't tell.* Really, this common rule is just an extension of the instruction above to revisit imagery. It's worth going through a poem or story, however, and circling or highlighting any abstractions or objects that could be described in concrete terms. Then question each of those marks. Should the abstraction be replaced with a concrete image? Could the idea of love be better demonstrated through an embrace or dialogue than through the use of the term?

- *Look again at the first line or sentence.* In fact, quite often, both poems and stories don't really "start" where the first draft begins. The syntax of the first line also sets the mood and tone and provokes an initial response from the reader. Just for the heck of it, try cutting the first sentence entirely—maybe even the first stanza or paragraph—and look at the piece again, as objectively as you can. If it doesn't work, put the material back.

- *Reconsider the ending.* Endings of creative pieces are tough. Unlike essays, which should clearly round off an argument, poems and stories don't always benefit from neatly packaged endings, but they also shouldn't trail off into meaninglessness. Spend some time on the imagery, syntax, and moment of the ending—is it appropriate, appealing, and meaningful?

- *Revisit the title, or, if the piece is untitled, consider giving it a title.* A pet peeve of mine: using the first or last line of a poem or story as a title. Not only does this smack of desperation, it robs the work of some of its strength. A trick you might consider in revision, however, is the idea of moving a detail out of the piece altogether and sticking it in the title. Look at how much time you can save—this is the first stanza of an untitled poem written by a high school senior:

Papa paints the walls *azul*,
the color of my brother's eyes.
Mama makes the tortillas
Her back hunches over the stone . . .

In the revision, the first line becomes the title, allowing us to see the central figure of the poem immediately. Here's the entire revised version:

While Papa Paints the Kitchen

Mama makes the tortillas
Her back hunches over the stone
Her feet cracked and grimey
She sings *"me encantan los ojos del azul"*

The kitchen is so hot
That the white linens of my mother's dress
Become transparent
And meld into her strong back

A bead of sweat drips from the tip of her nose
Mixes with the dirt floor
Mixes with the flour
Mixes with Papa's paint

She braids my hair
She sews my white linen clothes
She sings me songs about *mi hermano*

And I'm her *muchacha del piso de la suciedad*
Her dirt floor girl

—Zoë Etkin

- And, finally: *Don't fall in love with what you've written*. Treat your first drafts like blind dates, not love affairs. Think of all the ways you can improve them, or how much better the next one will be.

Poetry

Sometimes, out of desperation, I have students write really horrible poetry. Here's the formula: the poem must use simple rhyme, must contain the words *love, soul,* and *forever*, must use a metaphor that involves a river, rain, or eyes, should contain at least one inverted sentence ("my love for you will die not / like a river reaching into forever . . .") and one cliché, and should be printed in some flowery font and centered on the page. Sometimes I let the class throw in some more suggestions: we include a puppy or use the word *precious* in the title. You know what happens?

You get poems that sound like greeting cards?

Yup. And there's money to be made in greeting cards, so I won't knock it. But my students are a lot less likely to spend three or four bucks on one in the future, once they know the formula.

What I *hope* happens is that students learn some lessons about revising their own poems. Once they have drafts, I often suggest these approaches to revision:

- *Look for forced or contrived lines.* This is particularly important with rhyming poems, where a line that has to rhyme with the phrase "both of us" winds up in syntax more convoluted and out of context than a fish-flavored pretzel: "To get downtown I did ride the bus." In fact, since English is such a rhyme-poor language, I encourage students to avoid rhyme unless we're specifically working on that aspect of poetry. Even free verse poems may include contrivances, however; if a student tells you a line has to remain because he or she "really wanted to use it," that's a pretty good sign it should be cut.

- *Think about line breaks.* Line breaks in poetry have enormous power—they can emphasize or de-emphasize ideas, can change the rhythm and pacing of the poem, or can create or resolve ambiguity. Here's an easy exercise to prove it to students. Ask them to write the next line of this poem:

  At the bus station I find . . .

Then, after sharing some possibilities, discuss the momentary drama created by breaking the line after the word "find." The poem might continue, for instance, like this:

At the bus station I find
myself staring at other passengers,
listening to the rain.

I suggest having students look over a draft of a poem while asking them
to consider these specific aspects of line breaks:

- Have you broken the lines in ways that coincide with grammatical or
  syntactical units? If so, is there a good reason to do so (or not to)?
  Might *enjambment* (the practice of breaking lines in the middle of sentences or phrases, which often makes language sound less rhythmic
  and more conversational) create a flow you'd like more?

- Do any lines end with articles or prepositions, and if so, might these
  be better moved to the next line?

- Are there any spots where breaking the line differently would create
  an interesting ambiguity or alternate interpretation?

- Do your line breaks reinforce the visual aspects of the poem? Would a
  long, skinny poem make more sense for this topic than a short, fat
  one?

- Do your line breaks reinforce the tone of the speaker?

- *Condense and cut phrases and lines.* Poetry, especially, benefits from tight-
  ening; in general, the least number of words that can be used to express
  a thought, the better. Strong verbs often help with condensing, and condensing in turn leads to specificity; consider the difference between the
  line "I was driving to the local market to buy a newspaper" and "I
  fetched the paper from Graybar's."

- *Eliminate all "-ing" verbs, "-ly" modifiers, and "-tion"and "-ment" nouns.* Just
  another step in condensing language, these words can usually be replaced
  by stronger and more immediate diction: "I ran" instead of "I was running," "he stammered" instead of "he said haltingly," "he beamed" instead
  of "he beamed with satisfaction."

- *Expand the ending.* Great poems are secure in their endings; you feel this
  if you read them out loud, especially. Reconsider the ending of the
  poem. Does it pack a punch? Would a stronger image help? Could it be
  more detailed? Does it convey the meaning of the poem without seem-
  ing trite or too neatly packaged?

- *Improve the sound of the language.* Many amateur poets never even consider the music of a free verse poem, and many mature poets consider it

more in revision than in a first draft. Music doesn't come easily, but just as strong explications of poetry will consider sound and rhythm in any poem, strong poems will take sound into account during revision. Ask yourself what sounds reflect the content of the poem and its imagery, and look for words or phrases that fit those sounds. Ask, too, how syntax contributes to the overall rhythm and how that rhythm connects to the poem's meaning.

- *Ask yourself if the event of the poem is clear.* If there's not a clear situation in the poem, then you probably need more detail and concrete description. A poem without an event is like a story without a setting; it's possible to pull it off, but tough.

  Here, for instance, is an excerpt from a poem by a high school sophomore:

I'm hoping one day a train might come,
A cargo, or freighter, maybe a passenger
That will take me away.

The sentiment is fine, but if the poem started this way (as many student poems do) and never developed a story, setting, or event, I'd ask for one. Here, though, is how Dixie's poem actually starts—notice the power offered by the concrete setting, both in time and place:

Nanny doesn't like me to play
On the old broken down railroad tracks
On fall days with blue skies
The trees the color of red

She doesn't like it
When Elmwood Elementary ends
And I don't come home
She knows where I am

On the railroad tracks
Where no train has come along in years
No train would ever come
To broken down Packwood County

I'm hoping one day a train might come
A cargo, or freighter, maybe a passenger
That will take me away.
                                        —*Dixie Neely*

- *Ask yourself if the poem goes somewhere*. What is the change, development, or shift in the poem? Is it a journey? If not, what holds it together? (There are other possibilities for lyric poetry, such as sound or metaphor, but they're demanding.)

Fiction and Creative Nonfiction

The best way to ruin a good story is not to tell it. We love stories; we tell them all the time. The trick with writing a good story down is partly to get out of its way, to let the story tell itself. And that, weirdly, takes much more skill, craft, and deliberate creation than one might imagine.

We rarely tell stories, after all, in the way we wish to read them. Thus writing a story means considering how to frame dialogue, how to pace events, how to create characters—all of the decisions that can be glossed over in telling your best friend, for instance, about how you wrecked your car. Students can often get a story down in its basic form just by writing down a sequence of events—first I ran the red light, then I drove my car into a ditch—but crafting those events into a compelling story or personal narrative is more tricky. I suggest these tips to students when they're ready to revise their fiction or creative nonfiction:

- *Think about your audience*. I have a friend who reads bestsellers with a red pen in her hand; every now and then she stops and scribbles a furious note to the author, something along these lines: "What are you thinking? Don't describe characters by having them look in the mirror! How trite!" I'm not quite as bad; I enjoy a good thriller, and I think there are some essential techniques to writing such a work (fast pacing and plentiful dialogue, for instance). Students don't always seem to distinguish between genres, purposes, and audiences, however. A science fiction story, a work of literature for children, a literary story—all have different audiences, and those audiences have different tastes and expectations. Awareness of audience might affect paragraph length, diction, dialogue, characterization, and any number of other elements of a prose piece.

- *Consider adding or revising dialogue*. Beginning writers seem averse to using dialogue, sometimes when they need it most. Strong dialogue's not easy (trite dialogue is), but fiction often rests on the strength of what characters say. One revision strategy: take any paragraph of narration and turn it into dialogue. Have a character describe the setting instead of the narrator, or make getting from one place to another evident through conversation rather than strict narration.

- *Cut speaker tags*. Speaker tags are the short bits of narration that identify the character who has just spoken or is about to: "she said," "he answered," "she shouted." Much of the time, speaker tags can just go. When they must remain, either for rhythm or because without them it wouldn't be clear who has said what, most contemporary writers strive to make them as innocuous as possible, avoiding such amateur verbs as "he expostulated" or "she whined irritably." Both the whining and its irritability ought to be clear from the dialogue itself.

- *Cut repetition and extra words in sentences.* Like poetry, prose often benefits from efforts to condense. That last sentence, for example, originally read, "As with poetry, students often help their prose when they make efforts to condense the language." See?

- *Reconsider point of view.* I recently spoke to a novelist who is rewriting an entire book-length manuscript. "It's the main character's story," she told me, "but it turns out that the best friend has to tell it." First person, third person, one narrator, many—there are numerous choices to be made in fiction about who presents information, how much access he or she has to it, and how reliable he or she is as a narrator. Try rewriting a section of the story from a completely different point of view just to see how it works.

- *Compare the chronological order of events with the psychological or emotional order.* Most of us learned about the "climax" of a story early on. Some stories, though, have more than one climax—the emotional climax is not necessarily the same as the moment of greatest action. Keeping both in mind can make a better plan and resulting story. Where do the key moments fall in your story? Is there more than one key moment and, if so, should they fall at the same place?

- *Change the "lens" and focus.* Imagine your story being filmed—where would the camera be? Would the reader see a wide shot or a close-up? Would the camera move or shift angles? Sometimes moving the narrative camera, changing the lens distance or focus, for instance, can resolve problems in a scene or entire story.

- *Question the timing and pacing of events.* One of the most difficult aspects of a story involves getting characters from one place to another or from one time to another. Pacing matters; does the drive home, for instance, seem interminable or ridiculously short? In many cases, the goal is to describe such shifts in such a way that readers don't even question the veracity of events. Revisit transitional scenes or moments in your story and ask if they could be more fluid.

- *Roll your characters around to see if they're round or flat.* Here's a question: do the characters you intend to be fully developed do anything that surprises you but then makes sense? Round characters are like real people; they act and react in ways that aren't quite predictable but are in character; flat characters are in character all of the time but never surprise. Reconsider your character's action, decisions, and words to see if they feel "real."

Read the following excerpt from a story that went through several revisions. In the end, Leah, a high school freshman, managed to create the character, the pacing, and the focus of the story all to her satisfaction by starting the story in the character's bathroom with an emphasis on everyday tasks:

> Warm water, sent by her jittery hands, nudged her closed eyelids and they cautiously opened. She flipped the light switch with her wet left hand and avoided making eye contact with herself in the mirror. She had no idea how long it had been since she wandered, while sluggishly hitting the walls, from her bedroom to where she stood now. The toothpaste tasted odd today. Her hairbrush's bristles, wound with brown curls, caressed her scalp and gave her a moment of silence like a cat cleaning his fur. She had taken a shower the night before, but her hair was still moist and smelled of wet leaves. Tucked between the mirror and the wall behind there was a Latin award—"Carpe Diem" was written in big cursive letters. Her name was printed underneath and a stamp of the principal's signature ran under that. Still getting the knots out, she walked into her dark room.
>
> —*Leah Shapiro*

Leah resists the easy temptation to have this character describe herself by looking in the mirror—instead, we learn more about the character's emotional state from her refusal to look and we learn a bit about her appearance from the description of a hairbrush. One simple sentence, "the toothpaste tasted odd today," breaks the rhythm of longer syntax and drives home an impression of the teenage character, as does the juxtaposition of the Latin award and the character's physical disorientation and disorder.

- *Lie*. Fiction and creative nonfiction are largely about the details one selects and how they're presented. Different details; different meaning. Some writers, though, find themselves locked in to real events in creative nonfiction and afraid to draw on real experience—but also to change it—for fiction. Convincing yourself to lie in order to tell the truth is an important part of helping develop your skill as a storyteller.

Revising Throughout the Process of Writing

Much of what I've written in this book about revising essays applies to revising creative writing, as well. But I also believe that the creative writing classroom or class period should look and feel a little different from other classes. Stories and poems can be intensely personal, both in what they reveal and in how they're expressed. Because of this, I suggest some specific guidelines for working through the process of creative writing with students and responding to that writing.

To begin with, responses to creative pieces, I believe, must emphasize positive aspects of a piece and progress by the writer. Learning to write is an ongoing process; you don't master it and you never feel secure. Students will make mistakes and will learn from them over time—revision, therefore, requires a process that focuses on learning the craft as much as on rewriting a single work:

- *Offer students numerous models and encourage emulation.* Include models by students and writers the students may not have heard of, and make the models contemporary. Who wants to be faced with a Wordsworth poem or a passage of Henry James every time you get a creative writing assignment? Make models accessible, and allow discussion to have a limited focus. You don't need to analyze the model as you would in a literature class; a few points about craft may be enough to get a student writing.

- *Focus on workshopping rather than peer editing.* The difference? Peer editing has a singular goal: to improve the piece. A good student workshop, I believe, is one in which every member treats each piece of writing as if it were his or her own. Suggestions are made with an eye for clarity and communication, strengths are pointed out, and discussion takes place about overall strategy and craft. I like workshopping groups to be enjoyable, casual, and nonthreatening.

- *Fast-write often.* In addition to frequent fast-writing sessions, in which students have the opportunity to put words on the page without concern that they'll be graded down for errors or for being off-topic, reviewing fast-writing and writing again from scratch works well. Looping, too, is particularly effective for fiction, in which entire stories might emerge from a single detail in a first draft.

- *Celebrate success—and failure.* Publication offers a source of validation for students. But even poems and stories that aren't destined to take first place in a competition or to appear in print are part of a roadmap toward learning to write, and may well serve a writer well in the future. Try having students keep portfolios and revisit them often to discuss progress, try new approaches to old ideas, or rework previous pieces in new forms.

When it comes to revision, creative writing sometimes benefits from strategies that might not work with essay writing. Consider asking students to try some of the following revision techniques with their poems and stories:

- *Rewrite without looking at the original.* I've never known anyone who *wanted* to rewrite an analytical essay from scratch, though I've had several students who had to do so—one wrote ten pages and then ran over her laptop with a car. Poetry, in particular, sometimes benefits from this approach. Shelve the first draft and write the poem again without even looking at what you wrote before—eventually it may be some combination of the two versions that you stick with.

- *Rearrange randomly and see what happens.* With word processing, rearranging pieces of stories and poems is easier than ever. Take advantage of it—jumble paragraphs from a story and stick them together in odd ways, then go back and see if you can make the story make sense. Sometimes new angles and structures for storytelling open up, leading to even more revision.

- *Change the structure entirely.* Try writing a free verse poem as a sonnet, or a sonnet as a series of haiku. Form and structure can inhibit beginning writers, but they also sometimes allow new ideas to spring forth, ways of looking at and hearing words one wouldn't have considered without the form. You can always go back to the original version, after all.

- *Map the story.* Draw a literal, physical map of the story's plot (or the events in a poem). Then fill in the map with details that aren't in the story, whether your map takes you from one state to another or from the back door of a house to the living room. Consider adding some of those details into the revision.

Poets and authors have concocted hundreds of ways of tricking themselves into writing and rewriting. Writers find little strategies for forcing themselves to work, because it's so easy not to—I know a poet who takes a friend to lunch once for every week he doesn't produce a poem, and another writer who tells his wife not to let him eat until he's written five hundred words—but as easy as it is to avoid writing, sometimes it's worse not to. Students can have a luxury not afforded to many professionals, however—time and space in which to write, freedom to experiment, and a built-in response network. It can still be hard for them to force themselves toward creativity; much of the teacher's job, I think, is making that process and the revision that follows a little bit less daunting. If we can make writing fun and profitable (not in dollars but in satisfaction), we'll help to create lifelong writers as well as better readers.

Appendix A

A Sample Plan for Teaching Revision in a Semester

This book offers many ideas and strategies. I sometimes get overwhelmed thinking about all of the tools my students need but don't have, and as a result I either try to teach too much, too quickly, or too little overall. That's when I start making plans.

This schedule is a sample, of course, not an absolute prescription. It's meant to augment the study of literature, grammar, or other aspects of the language arts curriculum you might teach. It's also meant to be a fluid plan—I've marked the end of six- and nine-week grading periods (one or the other is used by many secondary schools), and I've mentioned the chapters where you'll find exercises that might enhance your lessons at each stage. The list also needs to be adapted for the grade level you teach (for a middle school teacher, for instance, four essays in a semester might be rather ambitious) and the challenges your students face. Take this schedule as a starting place—the revision of it is up to you.

Stage	Revision Focus	Where to Find Ideas
Week 1	Have students design essay topics (use summer reading or a new work)	Chapter 2
	Discuss audience and purpose	Chapter 2
Week 2	Design a thesis and introduction	Chapter 2
	Revise the introduction in pairs or groups	Chapter 4
Week 3	Write essay one (first draft)	
	Review and improve the use of evidence	Chapter 2
	Review and improve organization	Chapter 2
Week 4	Revise the conclusion of essay one (in pairs or groups)	Chapters 2, 4
	Plan essay two (topic, thesis)	Chapter 2

Week 5	Design and write essay two	
	Discuss revision of style using essay one: basic syntax, worst offenders	Chapter 3
Week 6	Final draft of essay one	
	Revise essay two (organization, evidence)	Chapter 2

End of six weeks

Week 7	Revise essay two (basic style)	Chapter 3
Week 8	Essay two final draft	
	Discuss and plan on-demand writing	Chapter 5
Week 9	Write an on-demand essay	Chapter 5
	Practice on-demand revision	Chapter 5

End of nine weeks

Week 10	Creative writing—writing and initial drafts	Chapter 7
Week 11	Creative writing—revision	Chapter 7
Week 12	Essay three—planning and first draft	Chapter 2
	Creative writing—publication/presentation	Chapters 4, 7
	Practice advanced syntax exercises	Chapter 3

End of six weeks (2)

Week 13	Essay three revision: content, style	Chapters 2, 3
	Practice advanced syntax and style	Chapter 3
Week 14	Final draft of essay three due	
Week 15	Essay four planning and rough draft	Chapter 2
Week 16	Essay four—work on voice, turns of phrase	Chapter 3
	Creative writing/on-demand essay practice	Chapters 5, 7
Week 17	Final draft of essay four due	
	Creative writing or on-demand revision	Chapters 4, 5, 7
	Discuss the requirements of a portfolio of work from the semester (use metacognition)	Chapter 4
Week 18	Semester Portfolio due	Chapter 4
	Publication or sharing with public audience	Chapter 4

End of six weeks (3)

End of nine weeks (2)

Appendix B

More About Research by Chris Thaiss

Over the last several years, Chris Thaiss and his colleague Terry Myers Zawacki, through a study conducted at George Mason University, have compiled a list of conclusions about student writing proficiency, practice, and assessment. Their surveys of writing teachers, students, and course materials has resulted in recommendations which are more fully explained in their book *Engaged Writers and Dynamic Disciplines: Research on the Academic Writing Life* (Heinemann, March 2006).

The recommendations that result from this research speak to the practices of college students, but for high school teachers preparing their students for a college environment the conclusions still ring true. Here, first, are the six conclusions (?) that resulted from the study:

- Good college writing comes from what writers care about.
- College writers must confront the tension between convention and individual desire.
- There are no simple rules for college writers—study the reader and the task.
- Everyone agrees on the terms, but they don't agree on the meanings.
- College writers move to proficiency through stages of development.
- Students credit responsive teachers for their growth as writers.

And, from these conclusions, come implications for writing teachers:

- Careful assignment design matters: students benefit from models, rubrics, and disciplinary examples of terms like *clear thesis* or *concise sentences*.
- When we ask for "original thinking" or "your own conclusions," we need to show what this might mean—especially in writing based on the research of others.

- We can benefit students by explaining the methods, scope, and discourses of our branches and research fields within the larger discipline.

- Feedback to students on their writing is crucial to student understanding of the discipline and the discourse.

- We should help students find and *express* their passions for learning within the assignments we give.

- We should give students opportunities to write reflectively on their growth as writers.

A brief explanation of each of the above conclusions and implications can also be found at the following website: http://mason.gmu.edu/%7Ecthaiss/ #Research.

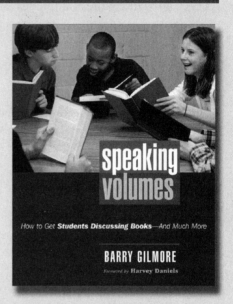